◆

The Black Dog
Summer on the Vineyard
Cookbook

◆

The Black Dog
SUMMER
~ ON THE ~
VINEYARD
COOK
BOOK

Joseph Hall and Elaine Sullivan

WITH

Jack Livingston, Charlie Esposito, and Doug Hewson

Photographs by Terry Pommett and Alison Shaw

Design by Kolodny & Rentschler

Little, Brown and Company

Boston   New York   London

Grateful acknowledgement is made to Sterling Publishing Co. Inc., for permission to quote from *Quotations with an Attitude* by Roy L. Stewart, ©1995, Sterling Publishing Co., Inc., NY, NY.

Grateful acknowledgement is made to Gibbs Smith, Publisher, for permission to quote from *Never Ask a Man the Size of His Spread* by Gladiola Montana (Salt Lake City: Gibbs Smith, Publisher, 1993).

Grateful acknowledgement is made to Indian Hill Press, for permission to use *Remembering Nancy Luce* Illustration and Verse ©1999 by Indian Hill Press

Black Dog Poster on page 1
by Dana Gaines ©1996 by The Black Dog

PHOTOGRAPHS BY:
Charlie Cole: page 150 · James Douglas: page 74
Bob Gothard: pages 1, 39, 68 · Bruce Mathews: page 71 · Tina Miller: page 6
©Terry Pommett: pages 2, 8, 12, 14, 15, 17, 22, 25, 29, 30, 31, 32, 36/37, 38, 42, 47, 49, 52, 56, 57, 60, 61, 62, 65, 66, 70, 72, 77, 82, 83, 84, 85, 87, 88, 90, 94, 98, 100/101, 103, 104, 106, 107, 114, 114, 120, 122, 123, 124, 129, 131, 132, 137, 141, 142, 144, 146, 152, 155, 157, 161, 166, 169, 173, 174, 176, 180, 183, 184, 187, 190, 193, 196, 199, 203, 204, 205, 208, 210
Mary Rentschler-Alley: pages 79 · Nancy Safford: page 1
©Alison Shaw: pages 10/11, 18, 19, 28, 40/41, 48, 54, 55, 67, 74, 78, 93, 112, 117, 126, 138, 148, 149, 164, 192, 194/195, 206, 209, 217
Peter Simon: pages 6, 9 · Nancy Tutko: page 165

The Black Dog® and logo are registered trademarks of The Black Dog Tavern Company, Inc.

Original Black Dog drawing by Stephanie Phelan, 1976

First Edition

ISBN 0-316-33932-6
Library of Congress Control Number 00-13110

10 9 8 7 6 5 4 3 2 1

RRD-W

Printed in the United States of America

Welcome

FOR NEARLY THREE DECADES, The Black Dog Tavern has welcomed Vineyarders and travelers looking for simply great food ~ three meals a day, seven days a week. The Tavern was named after "Black Dog," the much loved four-legged companion of Capt. Robert Douglas. We've tried to follow in our namesake's paw prints and be just as welcoming and unimpressed with celebrity as that rascal of a pup.

When you walk into our Tavern building, crafted of recycled nineteenth-century yellow pine and filled with nautical memorabilia, you'll see our cooking line. Our open kitchen is not new ~ it's been there from the beginning. When everything is fresh, from fish caught that morning to veggies picked that day at local farms, there's no reason to keep the kitchen closed off in a back room. Our patrons enjoy watching our cooks strut their stuff ~ flames, tavern bell, and all ~ and don't hesitate to add their suggestions to the mix. In many ways, this small family business has become everyone's Black Dog. Changes in the menu or the operation are debated around the wood stove by the regulars or in letters to the editor in the *Martha's Vineyard Times* or *Vineyard Gazette*. More often than not, our phone rings with questions from off-Island friends about Island events, or in search of a recommendation for lodging, or the phone number of another Island business. But then, in a resort community where restaurants come and go from season to season, The Black Dog has thrived and is now feeding a second generation of Islanders and visitors. Good will and warm feelings always help any restaurant, but that's not enough without the fundamental ingredient ~ good food.

For this, our first cookbook, we have chosen more than one hundred of our favorite summer recipes, included some cooking tips from the "kitchen gods" and flavored it all with a few of our tall tales and a little Island lore. We hope to bring a bit of the good tastes and good times we enjoy at The Black Dog to your kitchen.

Captain Douglas and Black Dog

"When you move to a town that doesn't have a good year~round restaurant, you have to build one! And we did!"

~ CAPT. ROBERT DOUGLAS

IN 1971, A RESTAURANT OPENED IN VINEYARD HAVEN on Martha's Vineyard in January. This was not exactly an auspicious time to open a dining establishment in an area known as a summer resort ~ but The Black Dog wasn't built to attract summer visitors. Now, nearly thirty years later, all of the tales of

The Black Dog Tavern's beginning seem to harken back to two things ~ a cannon and a bowl of good fish chowder.

The chowder's part of the tale is easy to explain. Most of the food establishments on the Vineyard closed right after Labor Day, and Islanders tended to look at the winter as the stay-at-home season.

If you didn't want to cook, or were looking for some entertainment and human contact, the options were slim to none. The idea of a place where you could enjoy a good bowl of fish chowder (Capt. Douglas's favorite) and sit around the fire exchanging stories had universal appeal, but it was just a matter of wistful conversation ~ until the cannon...

ROBERT DOUGLAS COLLECTS maritime memorabilia ~ ship models, half shells, and harpoons. You can see a lot of it on display inside The Black Dog. Sometime in the late 1960s he found a cannon at a wrecking yard outside of Boston. After service on some Civil War vessel it had been recycled as a bollard ~ nose down in the ground at the edge of a pier securing mooring lines from berthed ships. Being an astute observer and extremely knowledgeable about maritime history, Bob recognized how unusual it was to find such a cannon intact and he was determined to have it for his collection. Since this particular cannon weighed over 9,000 pounds, getting it to the Island became a challenge. The only truck capable of handling its weight at the wrecking yard was already loaded with salvaged pine. To get the cannon, Bob had to buy all that wood, and he did ~ 6,000 pounds of yellow pine for six cents a foot. As it turned out, the timber had an even longer pedigree than the cannon. The knot-free beams, salvaged from old mill buildings, were estimated to have been cut when the trees were at least 100 years old ~ trees that were saplings in the 1600s.

Since Bob Douglas already owned land along the waterfront, it was not long before the idea of The Black Dog Tavern was transformed from a rough sketch on a napkin to a building on the beach by master builder Allan Miller. Its size was determined by the number of yellow pine beams that came on the truck; its height was equal to half the length of the six longest beams. All of the yellow pine was used ~ "waste not, want not." The name of this new establishment was almost a foregone conclusion since Black Dog was Bob's ever-present four-legged companion, and "tavern" evoked all of those wistful visions of camaraderie and conversation. The fact that Vineyard Haven was, and is, a "dry" town never mattered.

From the beginning, The Black Dog Tavern occupied a place in the heart of the Island community ~ a combination of Yankee tradition and free-form fun that drew from the entire Vineyard talent pool, and beyond. Known as one of the Island's great cooks, Sally Knight was drafted immediately. She made chowder for The Black Dog at home and drove through Vineyard Haven with a large pot in the passenger seat of her car during the first few months of operation. Chefs from other Island restaurants came to cook on "special nights." Customers helped clear tables. During one crowded dinner, a fierce nor'easter at high tide broke a barge from its mooring in the harbor. As it was headed towards the Tavern, several "regulars" who happened to be there eating jumped up, unsolicited, grabbed some other diners, and tied the barge to the dock before it could smash into The Black Dog porch. The stories continue ~ cooks running out of the kitchen during lunch with fishing poles in hand, because they could see from the open kitchen the bluefish breaking the water at the end of the dock.

The Black Dog Tavern has been in continuous operation now for nearly thirty years. Even though our namesake, Black Dog, is gone, black dogs still wander around the beach and give rise to the question most often heard: "Is this THE black dog?"

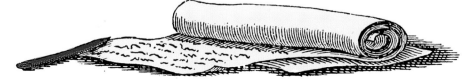

ACKNOWLEDGEMENTS

◆◆◆◆◆

IN RUNNING THE BLACK DOG for the last twenty years, I have been proud to work with and privileged to get to know a multitude of wonderful people who have contributed in countless ways to make The Black Dog a culinary and cultural icon. We have been lucky to attract outstanding talent, and some of the best have been around the longest. This, the first Black Dog cookbook, has been around a long time, at least in the hearts and minds of a dedicated few. I would like to give special acknowledgement and offer my sincere appreciation to Charlie Esposito, who has been in the kitchen and on the floor for more than 25 years; and to Jack Livingston, another 20-plus-year veteran, our most original executive chef (even though he disavows titles) and our overall culinary mentor. I would also like to applaud Doug Hewson, who interned at The Black Dog 15 years ago and returned just recently to take over our kitchens. And in particular, my deep gratitude goes to Elaine Sullivan, without whom this book would never have been seen. It has been Elaine's job to ride herd on all of us, to keep us in line and on target, and most of what you see and read (not just in this book, but in all our catalogs and media, since she took up the challenge here a dozen years ago) is a product of her handiwork and a result of her vision.

And hugs and kisses to my best friend and sweetheart, Susan Branch, who has fed and nurtured me and brought new vistas to my life. Finally, my heartfelt thanks to Bob and Charlene Douglas, for their friendship, trust, and consideration over all these years, and for starting it all.

~ Joe Hall

thank

ONE OF THE GREAT BENEFITS of doing The Black Dog cookbook is that it gives us an opportunity to celebrate and thank those who have contributed to the longevity and success of our growing business. The first note of thanks and praise must go to Captain Robert Douglas and his family for their vision and ongoing commitment to The Black Dog and the Vineyard community. There aren't many business owners who would allow their operation to run "in the red" every winter season. The Douglases do, to keep the staff employed and the Tavern open for conversation and fish chowder. Then there's Black Dog herself, our namesake, who helped inspire the enterprise and whose image has warmed the hearts of dog lovers everywhere over the years. Thanks and recognition are also due to Allan Miller, who masterminded the construction of the Tavern almost 30 years ago and operated the restaurant for the first three years.

From left: Jack Livingston, Doug Hewson, Elaine Sullivan, Joe Hall, Charlie Esposito

The Black Dog would never have continued without the positive energy and hard work of our crews over the years. One of the first can be seen in the old black and white photo taken by the fireplace years ago ~ our present staff is shown in the color photo at right wearing their "Last Crew of the 20th Century" shirts. Without the support of our customers over the years and the whole Island community, all of their effort would be unnecessary. We'd like to thank everyone who's visited The Black Dog for their support, from our old faithfuls who can be found at the table by the fireplace winter and summer, to those who are willing to stand in line and wait their turn during the hustle of summer.

Putting this cookbook together, like everything at

you...

The Black Dog, was far from a one-man or one-woman show. It took the cooperation of many, and the hard work of a few, starting with the faith and encouragement given us by John Taylor Williams, a/k/a "Ike," and the commitment of Jennifer Josephy, our very patient editor at Little, Brown. Translating recipes from "restaurant quantities" to home measurement, while maintaining flavor, wouldn't have been possible without the enthusiasm and frankness of the Black Dog crew, who tested all of the recipes in their home kitchens and let us know where we goofed and where we succeeded ~ this is their cookbook, too. We'd like to recognize the generosity of local Island merchants: Bramhall & Dunn, Le Roux Home, Midnight Farm, Rainy Day, Mariposa, In the Woods, Andrea Angevin, and Sylvia Thompson, who lent us dinnerware and accessories for our "food shots" after we'd exhausted our own home supplies.

If the photographs of our food in this book inspire you to try our recipes, it's thanks to the eye of Terry Pommet, whose talent and patience continue to amaze us. For the wonderful exterior shots capturing the spirit of the Vineyard ~ fishermen and farmers ~ we relied on Alison Shaw, nationally recognized for her skill with light and color. Thanks also to Bob Gothard, a professional in all circumstances. The "look" of the book was created by the design divas ~ Carol Kolodny and Mary Rentschler ~ who worked with us from concept to completion to make this book possible. Thanks to Clifford and Leah Dorr, our desktop wizard and his Muggle wife; Steve Rosseel, our production guru; Chris Decker, our saving grace; Dan Waters, a/k/a D.A.W. ~ a poet and a scholar; and Joyce Spooner, our historian. The Black Dog recipes in this book grew from the creative efforts of many Black Dog cooks over the years and have been refined by our cookbook team: thanks to Charlie Esposito for ideas, recipes, drawings, and good humor; thanks to Jack Livingston for recipes, stories, expertise, and joining the e-mail generation; thanks to Doug Hewson for recipes and quick answers. To our fearless leader, Joe Hall, thank you for your generosity of spirit, support, friendship, and encouragement through this effort and many others. It has been a privilege for all of us to participate in this project, and we hope we've captured a bit of the Black Dog for you to enjoy in your kitchen.

~ Elaine Sullivan

Original Black Dog Crew and Friends, 1971

The Black Dog Crew at the end-of-season softball game, 1999

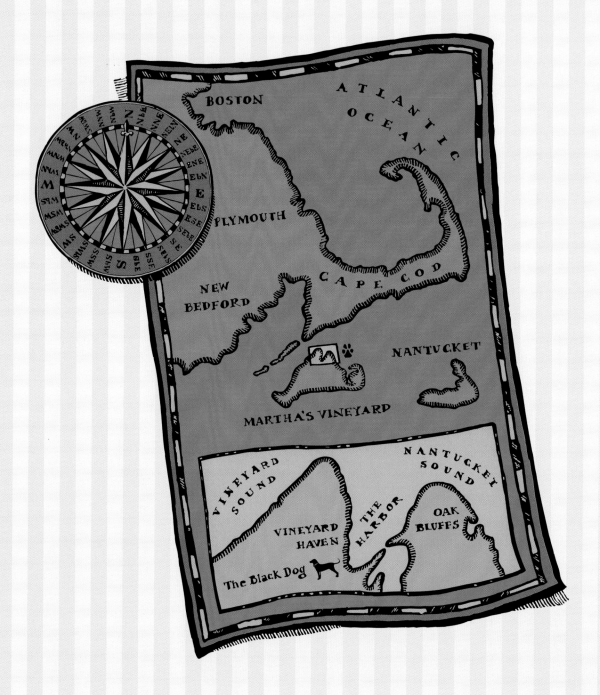

Table of Contents

◆ Black Dog Pantry ◆

THE BLACK DOG cooking philosophy is simple ~ find the freshest ingredients possible and prepare them in a way that is delicious, uncomplicated and pleasing to the eye. To us there are no "must do" rules in cooking ~ you can try anything once. When you write a changing daily menu for three meals a day, seven days a week, you have to be fairly inventive, but Black Dog food celebrates taste, not food fads. We have survived waves of nouvelle cuisine, blackening (Blackened Dogfish was a big hit), mesquite smoke with everything, hot sauces and raw cooked fish, but "tall food" never seemed very practical. Through it all we've continued to rely on butter and olive oil to enhance flavor, despite controversies.

As you read through this cookbook, we're sure you'll notice that there are several ingredients that reappear time and time again in various recipes. Black Dog cooks love fresh ginger and use it often, even in cookies. Sesame oil is another favorite. Here are some of our "must haves" for our pantry and walk-in fridge.

◆ Got to Have It Hot ◆

Hot chilis ~ we use poblano, jalapeños, and Thai chilis.

Chipotle Powder ~ a chipotle is a dried, smoked jalapeño. Get them whole and grind in a spice grinder, or buy powder.

Hot Chili Oil ~ a very spicy infused oil. Available in Asian markets, or steep dried red chilis in canola oil.

Ancho Powder ~ a dried poblano chili is called an ancho. Get them whole and grind in a spice grinder, or buy powder. Sweet-hot and wonderful in sauces.

Hot Bean Sauce ~ a traditional Asian ingredient made from ground beans and hot red chili paste. A little goes a long way.

Chili Paste ~ a paste of red chilis and garlic, crushed into a moist paste of Vietnamese origin. Very hot!

◆ Add to Your Veggie Basket ◆

Bok Choy ~ the greens and whites of the Chinese celery are both delicious and remain firm and succulent even when cooked.

Daikon Radish ~ a white elongated and pungent root, milder in flavor than its smaller red cousins.

Radicchio ~ red chicory. A delicate and somewhat bitter vegetable with bright red color that looks like a little red cabbage.

Broccoli Rabe ~ a dark, leafy and slightly bitter vegetable with smaller heads than traditional broccoli.

Jicama ~ a succulent, crisp and sweet root vegetable.

Shiitakes ~ tasty mushrooms, often dried for preservation. Plump them in liquid before using.

Tree Ears ~ also known as wood ears or cloud ears. An irregular-shaped Chinese fungus dried for preservation. Plump in liquid before using.

Lily Buds ~ the dried buds of the lily flower. Plump in liquid before using.

◆ Add Flavor With ◆

Coriander Seed ~ the seed of the herb also known as cilantro, it has a soft, nutty flavor.

Cumin Seed ~ used in curries and chilis. It has a warm flavor with a spicy aftertaste.

Dark Sesame Oil ~ very flavorful. Made from toasted sesame seeds, this flavorful oil has a low flash-point. Good for sautés and cold foods.

Ginger ~ a gift from the gods, it's fresh in root form. It has a sweet aroma and distinct pungent flavor, and is also used dried and ground.

Hoisin Sauce ~ Chinese bean sauce, flavored with garlic and chili.

Juniper Berries ~ the flavoring elements of gin, these dried berries from the evergreen shrub of the pine family lend great flavor to marinades.

Oyster Sauce ~ salty and sweet with an essence of oyster. Great for stir-fries, consistency slightly thick.

Pecan Meal ~ ground whole pecans with the consistency of coarse flour. Can be substituted for the flour used to "bread" chicken or fish.

Saké ~ Japanese rice wine, sweet or dry.

Salted Black Beans ~ these are fermented black beans which are dried with salt. Plump in water or stock before using.

Tahini ~ ground sesame paste. Mix well before using, as the oil will separate and rise to the top.

Tamari ~ natural Japanese-style soy sauce. Less salty than Chinese Soy.

◆ Gifts of the Sea ◆

Hijiki ~ calcium-rich seaweed. Also available dried.

Sea Bass ~ medium-texture, mild-flavored, white-fleshed fish. Two-to-three-pound fish served whole or as fillets. Similar fish would be grouper or rockfish.

Striped Bass ~ firm texture with a mild flavor. Mahi-mahi, sea bass, red snapper or perch are substitutes.

Bonito ~ medium-textured and full-flavored. Spanish mackerel or tuna are substitutes.

Cod ~ "the" sacred New England fish. Delicate to medium texture, mild flavor. Haddock, hake, or pollock are substitutes.

Flounder ~ delicate and mildly flavored. Substitutions are usually just other members of the flounder family: sole, fluke, plaice or dab. Remember that if a fish is lying on its side and both eyes are looking up at you ~ you have flounder.

Halibut ~ mild and firm-fleshed. Can substitute large cod, grouper, or snapper, although halibut's subtle flavor is distinct.

Atlantic Mackerel ~ oily, full-flavored with medium texture. Bluefish can be substituted.

Mahi-mahi ~ moderate flavor with medium firm flesh. Substitute striped bass, grouper or snapper.

Monkfish ~ mild-flavored and firm-textured. Often used as a substitute in stews for lobster or scallops.

Salmon ~ medium to full flavored, very rich with a medium texture. Trout or char are substitutes.

Mako shark ~ moderate flavor and firm texture. Often used as a substitute for swordfish or tuna.

Swordfish ~ firm fish with moderate flavor. Substitute halibut, shark, or tuna and use the same cooking techniques, but each has its own individual flavor.

Tuna ~ yellowfin, bluefin, and albacore. Moderate flavor and firm flesh. See swordfish above.

"Taste of the Vineyard"

EVERY SUMMER, The Black Dog, along with nearly sixty other Vineyard food establishments and beverage merchants, participates in an epicurean extravaganza known as Taste of the Vineyard.

Black Dog chefs love to "strut their stuff" and the competition can produce some delicious results. Those lucky enough to buy tickets enjoy the Island's best ~ all donated for the benefit of The Martha's Vineyard Preservation Trust. This fine organization, active on the Vineyard since 1946, has rescued, restored and preserved historic landmarks well known to Islanders and visitors alike. Properties under their care include The Flying Horses, the nation's oldest carousel, and the Vincent House, built in 1672, along with The Old Whaling Church and others. If you happen to visit our Island, try to include this wonderful (and tasty) event in your plans.

◆ ◆ ◆

Breakfast

Eggs

Specials

Morning Breads

*Start every day
off with a smile and
get it over with.*

~ W.C. FIELDS

OUR BREAKFAST COOKS start the day with a smile ~ often twisted ~ but sure to bring a laugh! Just read through our morning menu and you'll find big bountiful plates of Rasputin's Revenge (whole wheat pancakes with chocolate chips and strawberries doused with pure maple syrup, immortalizing one of our sugar-driven dishwashers) or Double Bypass (for a cholesterol-packed way to start the day) among the breakfast fare. Some breakfast entrée combinations, originally intended as an inside joke years ago, have won their place as favorite dishes ~ you'll find them in the following pages. So, picture yourself on the porch at The Black Dog, looking out on the vessels moored in Vineyard Haven harbor at the start of a summer day, and make yourself a sunny plate of Melancholy Babies (scrambled eggs with cauliflower and a side of melon). How about some fresh-squeezed OJ with that?

Eggs

Classic Black Dog Omelet

◆ ◆ ◆ ◆ ◆

Several years ago Manhasset Farm, up the road from the Tavern, was run by a bunch of well-intended hippies who would bring us vegetables whenever they had a surplus. We bartered produce for meals and had established a balanced symbiotic relationship until their broccoli crop came in, and in, and in. These big beautiful bunches overran our menu and we served broccoli with everything. A favorite was broccoli with eggs, the basis for the Classic Black Dog omelet.

1 tablespoon butter	½ cup broccoli, steamed and diced
3 eggs	½ cup of grated cheddar cheese
dash of salt and pepper	lots of Black Dog Sauce (see page 14)

1. Melt butter in skillet until frothy, while whisking eggs with salt and pepper.

2. Add egg mixture to pan. Shake pan back and forth until mixture is lightly set.

3. Now add the steamed broccoli, fold the omelet over, and continue cooking until lightly golden.

4. Serve smothered with warm Black Dog Sauce and sprinkled with cheddar cheese. If you don't have Black Dog Sauce on hand, you may substitute your favorite marinara sauce.

SERVES 1

All in the town were still asleep
When the sun came up with a shout and a leap.
In the lonely streets, unseen by man,
A little dog danced, and the day began.
~ RUPERT BROOKE

◆ Black Dog Sauce ◆

◆ ◆ ◆ ◆

When the restaurant first opened in '71, our cooks made a lot of chowder, day in and day out. Black Dog Sauce is an evolutionary creation that began when the cooks decided to go out on a limb and make something else. Tomato sauce seemed a good choice because of its versatility ~ you could put it on eggs, omelets, pasta, meats, or chicken. The best way to describe it is a chunky marinara, the chunks being whatever vegetables or herbs are fresh and available. Just make sure your tomatoes are really ripe and tasty. If not, substitute canned for better flavor. Ad lib to the basic recipe ~ we do!

¼ cup olive oil
1 cup diced onion
1 cup diced celery
1 cup diced carrot
8 to 10 ripe plum tomatoes,
    or one 28-ounce can of plum tomatoes,
    coarsely chopped
1 six ounce can of tomato paste
½ cup red wine
5 cloves garlic, minced
3 tablespoons chopped fresh oregano
    or 1 tablespoon dried
3 tablespoons chopped fresh basil
    or 1 tablespoon dried
1 bay leaf
salt and pepper

1. In a large saucepan, sauté the diced vegetables in the olive oil until tender.

2. Add the coarsely chopped tomatoes.

3. Add the tomato paste, wine, garlic, and herbs.

4. Simmer the sauce for one hour. Check the seasoning and add salt and pepper to taste.

MAKES ABOUT 6 CUPS

◆

◆ Manhassett Eggs ◆

◆ ◆ ◆ ◆ ◆

If flipping and folding omelets seems beyond your morning abilities, try this easy scrambled version of the Classic Black Dog Omelet on page 13. We often serve it with a side order of Black Dog Sauce, opposite.

1 tablespoon butter
3 eggs
dash of salt and pepper
½ cup broccoli, steamed and diced
½ cup cheddar cheese, grated

1. Melt butter in skillet until frothy. Whisk eggs with salt and pepper.

2. Pour beaten eggs into the melted butter. With a fork, stir eggs until they just begin to set.

3. Add the broccoli and cheese. Continue cooking until completely set and fluffy.

SERVES 1

◆

How to Flip an Omelet

1 Melt butter in an omelet pan and pour in three beaten eggs.

2 Tilt the pan while lifting eggs with a spatula.

3 Continue lifting as uncooked eggs flow under cooked eggs to form layers.

4 Continue lifting and cooking until eggs are firm.

5 Flip the egg to cook the other side. Afraid to flip? Slip the omelet onto a plate, then place the pan on top of the plate and invert to cook the other side. For a wetter omelet, omit this step.

6 Put onto plate while folding in half.

◆ Huey, Louie, Andouille ◆

◆ ◆ ◆ ◆ ◆

Maybe it's rising every day before the sun, or maybe it's a high caffeine intake or just a light heart, but Black Dog breakfast cooks know how to turn a phrase as well as an omelet when it comes to writing the menu. They have fun with items like Mother & Child Reunion (scrambled eggs with onions, peppers, and sautéed chicken) and combinations such as our Huey, Louie, Andouille omelet. But make no mistake, first the food has to be good, whatever the name.

1 tablespoon butter
3 eggs, beaten
salt and pepper
¼ cup sliced Andouille sausage
   (more if you like)

½ green bell pepper, cut in 1-inch pieces
¼ small onion, diced
your favorite salsa

1. Melt butter in skillet until frothy. In a separate bowl whisk eggs with salt and pepper.

2. Add onions and peppers to the pan and sauté for 1 to 2 minutes or until soft.

3. Add Andouille slices and sauté for another 1 to 2 minutes.

4. Pour in beaten eggs and shake until mixture is lightly set. Remember to keep the eggs moving by lifting the edges with a heavy-duty spatula.

5. Turn the omelet over, following directions on page 16.

6. Turn out onto plate and top with your favorite salsa or hot chili mixture.

SERVES 1

At The Black Dog we like to buy locally whenever possible. We get farm-fresh eggs from Debbie Farber, co-owner of Blackwater Farm in West Tisbury. Our irreverent crew, who have a habit of renaming everyone, have dubbed her "the chicken lady." True "salt of the earth," Debbie gives her chickens tender loving care and it shows.

◆ Farmer's Omelet ◆

◆ ◆ ◆ ◆ ◆

When you really want to break that fast, choose this omelet. It's full of flavor and substance. Plowing the north forty sounds possible after this hearty meal.

1 tablespoon butter
1 tablespoon chopped onion
1 tablespoon chopped bell pepper
2 tablespoons sliced, cooked new potatoes

3 eggs, beaten
1 tablespoon chopped, cooked breakfast sausage
1 tablespoon sour cream
1 tablespoon chopped scallion

1. In a medium skillet or omelet pan, melt the butter over medium high heat.

2. Add the chopped peppers and onions and cook for about 1 minute or until slightly soft. Add the cooked potato slices and brown on one side for about 2 minutes.

3. Now it's time to add the eggs and cooked sausage pieces.

4. Follow the basic omelet instructions on page 16, and remember to keep the eggs moving by lifting the edges. Continue cooking until solidified on the bottom.

5. Turn over and cook for another minute or so.

6. Fold onto plate and top with sour cream and scallions.

SERVES 1

◆ Double Bypass ◆

◆ ◆ ◆ ◆ ◆

A real heart-stopper ~ this is a favorite brunch order on Sunday when folks are on vacation and living large. When we see them arriving with bottles of champagne for Mimosas (remember, The Black Dog is in a dry town, so it's "bring your own") we know it's going to be one of those hollandaise mornings.

1 tablespoon butter
3 eggs, beaten
2 slices of cooked bacon, chopped
2 slices of avocado (approximately ¼ of a large avocado)
2 tablespoons grated medium cheddar cheese
2 tablespoons Easy Hollandaise Sauce (see page 26)

1. In a medium skillet or omelet pan, melt butter over medium high heat.

2. Add the eggs and cooked chopped bacon.

3. Keep the eggs moving by lifting the edges and continue to cook until solidified on the bottom.

4. Turn the omelet over to cook briefly on the other side and add the avocado and grated cheese. Continue to cook for about 30 seconds.

5. Fold onto plate and top with hollandaise sauce.

SERVES 1

◆

◆ Jack Went Fishing ◆

◆ ◆ ◆ ◆ ◆

At The Black Dog, Jack and fish are synonymous, hence the name of this omelet. You can substitute smoked Atlantic mackerel or other smoked fish for the smoked bluefish, since this Island treat is not always available across the country.

1 tablespoon butter
1 tablespoon chopped onion
3 eggs, beaten
2 tablespoons smoked bluefish pieces
1 tablespoon cream cheese
salt and pepper to taste

1. In a medium skillet or omelet pan, melt the butter over medium high heat.

2. Sauté the chopped onion for 2 to 3 minutes or until just browned.

3. Add the eggs and follow the basic omelet instructions on page 16, remembering to keep them moving by lifting the edges. Continue to cook until just solidified on the bottom.

4. Slip the omelet onto a plate, then place the pan on top of the plate and invert to cook the other side. For a wetter omelet, omit this step.

5. Add the bluefish and cream cheese and continue heating for another minute or so.

6. Fold onto a plate. Salt and pepper to taste.

SERVES 1

◆ Happy Heff ◆

◆ ◆ ◆ ◆ ◆

For over ten years, Jeff Heflin has been running the breakfast line at The Black Dog. At some point in the last decade, one of his cohorts created this scrambled combo, reflecting on Heff's less than cheerful a.m. mood ~ Happy Heff.

1 tablespoon butter
4 to 5 mushrooms, sliced thin
½ cup chopped fresh spinach
¼ cup chopped fresh tomato (1 small tomato)
5 eggs, beaten
salt and pepper
½ cup shredded cheddar cheese

1. Melt butter in a skillet or omelet pan until frothy.

2. Add the sliced mushrooms and sauté for about 1 to 2 minutes.

3. Toss in the spinach. It should wilt in about 1 minute.

4. Add the chopped tomato and sauté quickly to simmer any juice away. You don't want it to weep into the eggs.

5. Add the eggs and salt and pepper. Keep the eggs moving by shaking and swirling the pan. When they are about halfway firmed, add the shredded cheese.

6. Continue cooking until done.

SERVES 2

◆ Eggs in the Grass ◆

◆ ◆ ◆ ◆ ◆

Despite its resemblance to grass, asparagus belongs to the lily family. Maybe we should call this recipe "Eggs in the Flowers" ~ in any case, it's an elegant brunch for a lazy Sunday, or any day when time is your friend.

1 bunch asparagus
2 teaspoons white vinegar
½ cup Easy Hollandaise Sauce (see page 26)
4 eggs
2 English muffins, split and toasted
sliced strawberries

1. To prepare asparagus, bend each stalk at the base until tough fibrous ends snap off. Use a vegetable peeler to remove any remaining tough skin on thicker stalks. Boil or steam (your choice) until tender and bright spring green. Remove and rinse under cool water to stop the cooking process and retain color. Reserve.

2. Make Easy Hollandaise Sauce.

3. To poach eggs, fill a large saucepan with water and bring to a boil. Add white vinegar and reduce heat to a simmer. Crack and gently drop in eggs. Simmer for about 3 to 5 minutes. Remove when the whites are firm and the yolks are done to your taste.

4. To serve, arrange in layers starting with toasted muffins, then asparagus, eggs, and top with hollandaise. Garnish with sliced strawberries.

SERVES 2

◆

Martha's Vineyard TIMES

Vote Today in Edgartown, West...

Islanders in Force Take Beacon Hill

Legislators Hear Unified Opposition to New Bedford Initiative

Thursday, April 15, 1999

Volume 16, Issue No...

◆ Easy Hollandaise Sauce ◆

◆ ◆ ◆ ◆ ◆

This is a quick and delicious version of the classic sauce. Just make it and use it; hollandaise will separate if reheated.

2 egg yolks
1 tablespoon fresh lemon juice
1/4 pound (1 stick) butter, melted

splash Tabasco sauce
dash cayenne pepper
dash salt

Combine egg yolks and lemon juice in a food processor. Turn on and slowly pour in the melted butter. The sauce will emulsify. Season with Tabasco, salt, and cayenne pepper.

YIELDS: 1/2 CUP

◆

◆ Prairie Dog Scramble ◆

◆ ◆ ◆ ◆ ◆

This tasty version of steak and eggs cooks quickly in one pan. It has all the right stuff ~ you decide if you need a little A-1 on the table.

1 tablespoon butter
¼ cup trimmed sirloin tips, in ½-inch dice
salt and pepper to taste
1 tablespoon chopped onion
1 tablespoon chopped bell pepper
3 eggs, beaten

1. In a medium skillet or omelet pan, melt the butter over medium high heat.

2. Add the sirloin, season with salt and pepper, and cook for about 2 minutes.

3. Now add the onion and bell pepper and sauté for another 1 to 2 minutes to soften.

4. Pour in the beaten eggs, swirl pan and continue to keep eggs moving this way until set in a soft scramble.

5. Serve with Homefries, see page 29.

SERVES 1

Specials

Breakfast Sausage

❖ ❖ ❖ ❖ ❖

Buying whole pork loins allows us to be creative with the ends of the meat that won't be used as a center roast or cut up into pork chops. You can marinate the large ends whole for use in Oriental dishes, trim the chunks into bite-size pieces for stir-fries, or take the chunks and grind them to make sausage. Our breakfast sausage is made daily and is mildly spiced. You can add more spices like garlic, fennel, or crushed red pepper for more zest.

1 pound ground pork loin
1 teaspoon salt
½ teaspoon pepper
1 teaspoon dried sage or 5 fresh leaves, chopped
¼ teaspoon dried thyme
dash cayenne

Mix together well and form into patties. You should be able to make 10 to 12, depending on size. Fry about five minutes per side.

SERVES 4 TO 6

❖ Homefries ❖

❖ ❖ ❖ ❖ ❖

The secret to tasty homefries is to bake the potatoes, rather than to boil them ~ that way the flavor stays within the potatoes. At The Black Dog we bake trays of potatoes until they are just getting soft and let them cool. Our homefries are cooked in salted butter because we serve a lot of vegetarians, but in your own kitchen you can use some bacon fat for more flavor if you prefer. Want homefries in the morning? Just bake your potatoes the night before and refrigerate them.

3 baked potatoes
3 tablespoons of butter (or bacon fat)
1 small white onion, diced
salt and pepper

1. Chop the baked potatoes, skins and all, into 1-inch cubes. Reserve.

2. Melt the butter (or bacon fat) and add the diced onions. Sauté for about 2 minutes, then toss in the cut up potatoes.

3. Add salt and pepper and stir the mixture over medium heat for about ten minutes.

4. Serve hot and crispy.

SERVES 4

◆ Black Dog Fishcakes ◆

◆ ◆ ◆ ◆ ◆

Fishcakes are popular daily breakfast fare at **The Black Dog**. A delicious alternative to bacon or sausage, fishcakes follow the old Yankee tradition of wasting nothing ~ add a little cod, and last night's potato becomes today's breakfast. These fishcakes are far from frugal and very tasty.

2 cups cooked potatoes, mashed
1 pound skinless and boneless codfish
1 cup diced yellow onion
1 tablespoon fresh chopped thyme
  (or 1 teaspoon dried thyme)

1 teaspoon white pepper
1 to 2 teaspoons salt
1 egg, beaten
½ cup cream
2 tablespoons butter

1. If you don't have cooked potatoes on hand, cut up two large potatoes, unpeeled, and boil them in salted water for about 20 minutes until soft. Mash and reserve.

2. Place the fish in a steamer and top with the diced onion and seasonings. Cover and steam for about 10 to 15 minutes or until the onion is cooked.

3. In a medium-size bowl, combine the cooked fish and seasoned onions with the mashed potatoes. Mix in the egg and cream and form into 4 patties.

4. Sauté the fishcakes in butter until browned.

SERVES 4

Fishcakes Deluxe

◆ ◆ ◆ ◆ ◆

In the summer, one of our favorite ways to serve fishcakes at the The Black Dog is to top them with really ripe beefsteak tomatoes and cheese. Great for brunch with Gin Bloody Marys!

4 Black Dog Fishcakes, see above
4 slices beefsteak tomatoes
4 slices Muenster cheese

Prepare the fishcakes and top each with a large slice of ripe tomato and cheese. Place under a broiler to melt the cheese slightly and serve.

SERVES 4

◆ Thank George's Bank ◆

◆ ◆ ◆ ◆ ◆

For hundreds of years, fishermen have headed to George's Bank for cod, haddock, flounder, scallops, swordfish, tuna, and more. This large shallow bank on the outer continental shelf of North America, separating the Gulf of Maine from the open Atlantic, is now strictly controlled in the hope that the fish stocks can recover to their once fertile levels. Here in the land of the "bean and the cod," it's only fitting to honor this fishing ground. This recipe is not for the faint of heart.

4 Black Dog Fishcakes (See recipe on opposite page)
2 teaspoons white vinegar
4 eggs for poaching
½ cup Easy Hollandaise (See recipe on page 26)
your favorite toast

1. Prepare the fishcakes and keep warm.

2. Make hollandaise sauce.

3. To poach your eggs, fill a large saucepan with water and bring to a boil. Add white vinegar and reduce heat to a simmer. Crack and gently drop in your eggs. Simmer for 3 to 5 minutes. Remove when the whites are firm and the yolks are done to your taste.

4. For each serving, place a poached egg on a fishcake, cover with hollandaise sauce, and serve with toast on the side.

SERVES 2

◆

◆ "M" go Blue ◆
BANANA ~ BLUEBERRY PANCAKES

◆ ◆ ◆ ◆ ◆

With the summer season, The Black Dog's crew nearly doubles, adding students from across the U.S.A. and even across the pond. Some come to work just one season ~ others return for several summers. Each leaves memories behind with us. The name of our delicious Banana-Blues recalls a University of Michigan yell.

DRY INGREDIENTS
¾ cup unbleached all-purpose flour
¼ cup buckwheat flour
¼ cup whole wheat flour
2 tablespoons cornmeal (optional)
1 tablespoon sugar
1½ teaspoons baking powder
½ teaspoon baking soda
½ teaspoon salt
1½ teaspoons cinnamon

WET INGREDIENTS
2 eggs
2 tablespoons melted butter
1 to 1½ cups of whole milk

1 cup fresh blueberries
1 thinly sliced banana

favorite variation:

Rasputin's Revenge
(Named after one of The
Black Dog's best dishwashers)

To the basic batter add:
½ cup sliced strawberries and
¼ cup chocolate chips

◆

1. Mix the dry ingredients together in a medium size bowl.

2. In a separate bowl beat the eggs with one cup of milk and the melted butter.

3. Add this wet mixture to your dry ingredients until you have a basic pancake batter. Add the additional ½ cup of milk if the mixture is too thick, but don't stir too much or pancakes will be tough.

4. When the batter is ready gently fold in the blueberries.

5. Heat a griddle, adding a little clarified butter or oil. Ladle a five inch circle of batter onto the griddle. Drop a few slices of banana into each circle. Cook pancakes until the tops are covered with tiny bubbles, then flip them over and finish cooking.

6. Serve hot, with butter and pure maple syrup.

SERVES 4

Morning Breads

◆ Blueberry Butter Cake ◆

Super moist and loaded with wonderful summer blueberries ~ just add a pot of coffee and the Sunday paper and enjoy!

CAKE
2¾ cups all-purpose flour
1 cup sugar
1 tablespoon baking powder
½ teaspoon baking soda
½ teaspoon salt
3 eggs, beaten
1 cup buttermilk

1 cup melted butter
1 tablespoon pure vanilla extract
3 cups fresh blueberries

TOPPING
½ cup sugar
¼ cup flour
¼ pound cold butter, cut in bits
½ tablespoon ground cinnamon

1. Preheat the oven to 350°F. Butter and flour a 9 x 13-inch baking pan.

2. Sift the dry cake ingredients together onto a large square of waxed paper.

3. In a large bowl, mix together all the wet ingredients except the blueberries. Pour the dry ingredients into the wet and mix until just blended.

4. Pour the batter into the prepared pan and sprinkle with all of the fresh blueberries.

5. In a small bowl crumble together the topping ingredients. It's easy and mixes best if you use your hands. Sprinkle the topping over the batter.

6. Bake for about 50 minutes or until a knife comes out clean. The cake should be moist, not dry. After cooling, cut into big squares or small rectangles ~ your choice.

SERVES 10 TO 12

Whole Wheat
Banana Blueberry Muffins

◆ ◆ ◆ ◆ ◆

One of our most popular muffins ~ not too sweet and loaded with fruit and flavor ~ they make a great grab-and-run breakfast. You can mix the batter and refrigerate overnight. In the morning fold in fresh blueberries, bake, and enjoy!

2½ cups whole wheat flour
1½ cups rolled oats
2 teaspoons baking soda
⅛ teaspoon salt
¼ teaspoon ground mace or nutmeg

1 cup honey
1 cup canola oil
6 mashed ripe bananas
1 tablespoon pure vanilla extract
2 cups fresh blueberries

1. Combine dry ingredients in a large bowl. (If you don't have mace on hand, substitute nutmeg.)

2. In a separate bowl blend together the honey, oil, bananas, and vanilla.

3. Add the wet ingredients to the dry ingredients mixing only until the ingredients are combined. A good muffin batter should be lumpy. Cover and refrigerate overnight or proceed to bake now.

4. To bake, set your oven at 350°F. While it preheats, bring your batter to room temperature and grease and flour muffin tins. If you prefer, you may use liners.

5. Gently fold the blueberries into the batter. Fill each muffin cup at least ¾ full. These muffins do not rise very much.

6. Bake for about thirty to forty-five minutes. Test with a knife. The point should come out clean when the muffins are ready.

MAKES 16 TO 20 MUFFINS

*The average person's
need for sleep is
approximately
five more minutes.*

~ ANONYMOUS

Cranberry Tea Bread

◆ ◆ ◆ ◆ ◆

Serve this moist bread with your morning coffee and you'll enjoy the sweet-tart taste of oranges and cranberries. We use walnuts in our recipe, but you may substitute pecans or almonds if you prefer.

2 cups all-purpose flour
1½ teaspoons baking powder
½ teaspoon baking soda
1 teaspoon salt
1 cup sugar
4 tablespoons butter, softened
2 eggs
¾ cup fresh orange juice
orange rind (from about ⅓ of an orange)
¾ cup walnuts
1 cup cranberries (fresh or frozen)

1. Preheat the oven to 350°F and butter and flour an 8 x 4 x 2-inch loaf pan. Sift together the flour, baking powder, baking soda, and salt and set aside.

2. In another bowl, cream together the sugar and the butter with a wooden spoon or electric mixer. Add the eggs and mix well. Add the orange juice and the sifted dry ingredients and stir together.

3. Chop the orange rind in a small food processor for a few seconds, then add the walnuts and cranberries and continue processing until the nuts are just chopped. The orange rind should be in a fine mince.

4. Add this chopped mixture to the batter and stir until distributed. Pour into your prepared loaf pan.

5. Bake for about an hour. Check to see if a knife comes out clean at 45 to 50 minutes.

6. Cool on a rack for about 20 minutes before slicing.

SERVES 6 TO 8

◆

Maple Apple Cake

◆◆◆◆◆

On a cool summer morning treat yourself to a square of this dense, moist cake. It keeps well, so you can enjoy it all weekend ~ or as long as it lasts!

DRY INGREDIENTS
1½ cups unbleached flour
1½ cups whole wheat pastry flour
1¾ teaspoons baking powder
1¾ teaspoons baking soda
⅓ teaspoon ground nutmeg
1 tablespoon ground cinnamon

WET INGREDIENTS
½ cup plus 2 tablespoons butter, melted
1¼ cups maple syrup
3 eggs, beaten
2 tablespoons vanilla
⅔ cup buttermilk
2½ cups roughly chopped Granny Smith apples

TOPPING
1 cup unbleached flour
½ cup cold butter
¾ cup brown sugar

1. Preheat oven to 350°F and butter an 8 x 12-inch baking pan.

2. Sift the dry ingredients together on a large square of waxed paper.

3. In a large bowl combine the wet ingredients except apples.

4. Add the sifted dry ingredients to the bowl and mix just enough to blend. Add apples. Do not overmix.

6. Pour the batter into the prepared buttered pan.

7. In a small bowl, blend the topping mixture together until it crumbles. This is easy to do with your hands, or use a pastry blender.

8. Sprinkle the topping mixture over the batter.

9. Bake for about 50 minutes. Cool and cut into squares.

SERVES 10 TO 12 ◆

◆ Cranberry Almond Scones ◆

◆ ◆ ◆ ◆ ◆

Rich and buttery, these scones are delicious on their own or served with your favorite jam. At The Black Dog Bakery we bake them singly or in rounds, depending on how many we are producing. This recipe instructs you to form them into rounds, but if you are in a hurry you can drop the batter by large spoonfuls on a greased baking sheet and decrease the baking time to 12 to 15 minutes.

3½ cups all-purpose flour
4½ teaspoons baking powder
1 teaspoon salt
3 tablespoons sugar
½ cup cold butter

3 eggs
⅔ cup light cream
¾ cup fresh cranberries
½ cup toasted sliced almonds

1. Preheat oven to 425°F.

2. Sift together the dry ingredients into a large bowl. With a pastry blender, cut in the butter until the mixture is granular in appearance.

3. In a separate bowl beat the eggs until fluffy, then stir in the light cream.

4. Make a well in the center of the dry ingredients and pour in the egg mixture. Drop in the cranberries and the almonds, reserving some almond slices to sprinkle on top before baking.

5. Gently mix the wet and dry ingredients together into loose dough. Do not overmix.

6. Drop the dough on a lightly floured board, knead briefly and divide into two equal portions. Form these into two rounds, patting down to a thickness of about 3/4 inch. Place together on a greased baking sheet.

7. Sprinkle the top of each round with the reserved toasted almond slices and score the rounds with a knife into 6 wedges.

8. Bake for about 15 to 18 minutes or until a knife inserted comes out clean and the tops are lightly brown.

9. Remove to a rack to cool briefly. Serve warm.

YIELD: 12 TO 16

Lunch

Lunch at The Black Dog is a bustling affair. It's also the time when the crew is most likely to hear a phrase that sells Tums all over the Island: "I've got a ferry to catch." One amazing fact about the Vineyard is that we have no Golden Arches, no Whoppers, no drive-thru-window food dispensaries. Sitting down to a bowl of steamers, hand-cut fries, or Island greens may take a few minutes more, but we're sure it's better for your spirit.

Soups

Salads

Pasta

Specials

Do not make a stingy sandwich
Pile the cold-cuts high
Customers should see salami
Coming through the rye.

~ ALLAN SHERMAN

◆ Soups ◆

THE SECRET OF GOOD SOUPS is in the stock. To create flavorful soup, you need a good rich stock as your foundation. You can use water and the soup will be adequate, but usually it will lack character and be, well, watery. Stocks are fairly simple to make; they just take a little time. You can buy canned stock or flavored bases to save time, but there is really no substitute for making your own. What we do at The Black Dog is to start with the best basic ingredients and proceed. You want to make chicken soup, you go buy a really fresh chicken.

◆ Basic Fish Stock ◆

◆ ◆ ◆ ◆ ◆

Because we buy whole fish, sometimes more than 300 pounds a day, we have lots of fish bones available. You can get them at any good fish market; just ask.

3 tablespoons canola oil
1 large white onion
2 stalks celery
2 carrots
3 pounds white fish bones (a mix of flounder, haddock, halibut and cod, if possible)

1 teaspoon whole peppercorns
1 small bunch parsley
3 quarts cold water
1 tablespoon salt

1. Roughly chop the vegetables.

2. Heat a large, heavy-bottomed stockpot and add the oil. Add the vegetables and stir occasionally until they become transparent.

3. Place the fish bones on top of the vegetables, add the peppercorns, parsley, and salt, and cover with the cold water.

4. Bring the stock to a boil and skim any foam that rises to the top.

5. Lower the heat and simmer uncovered for 20 minutes.

6. Strain through a fine colander. Use within three days or freeze for later use.

YIELDS: 3 QUARTS

Basic Chicken Stock

◆ ◆ ◆ ◆ ◆

To make a clear chicken stock, take a chicken or chicken parts, but not the livers, and simmer. Jack actually raises chickens at home, so if he starts getting a cold, the Queen (his significant other) goes out back and butchers a bird to make stock ~ now that's basic.

1 whole chicken, 4 to 5 pounds
1½ teaspoons salt
fresh ground black pepper
1 large onion or 2 small onions, chopped
2 large carrots
3 stalks celery
2 bay leaves

1. Take the chicken, remove the giblets, if any. Rinse the bird and place in a large, heavy-bottomed pot. Cover with water and add salt and pepper.

2. Bring to a boil and simmer for 20 to 25 minutes. Skim pot as necessary to remove foam.

3. Remove the pot from heat and remove chicken to cool. Reserve liquid in pot.

4. When the chicken is cool enough to handle, remove all the meat and reserve. You can use this meat to make a chicken salad or chicken soup, once your stock is finished. Chop the bones and skin and return them, along with any meat that may adhere to the bones, to the pot.

5. Add vegetables and bay leaves. Return to boil, then simmer for at least 2 hours. You can simmer longer. When done, strain the broth, discarding all the bones, skin, and veggies. You can chill the broth and de-fat after chilling (don't remove all the fat because it carries the flavor). You can freeze any stock that you don't need immediately.

YIELDS: 3 QUARTS

Basic Vegetable Stock

◆ ◆ ◆ ◆ ◆

For veggie soups or sauces, it's great to have some vegetable stock on hand. It has very similar ingredients to our other stock recipes; the main difference is that you do not cook it as long.

2 teaspoons canola oil
2 carrots
2 to 3 celery ribs
1 large white onion
any fresh vegetable trimmings or
   scraps you have on hand
1 tomato, optional
8 cups water
2 bay leaves
2 teaspoons black peppercorns
2 to 3 sprigs fresh thyme
1 tablespoon salt
2 to 3 sprigs fresh parsley

1. Heat a large heavy-bottomed stockpot. Add oil.

2. Rough chop all the veggies in 1-inch pieces, and add to the pot. Add any veggie trimmings you may have on hand. Sauté until the onion is soft.

3. Add the water and seasonings and bring to a boil.

4. Reduce to a simmer and cook for 25 minutes.

5. Strain the vegetable broth through a sieve and use in soups or sauces.

YIELDS: 2 QUARTS

I'm not a vegetarian
because I love animals,
I'm a vegetarian
because I hate plants.

~ A. WHITNEY BROWN

◆ B.D. Quahog Chowder ◆

◆ ◆ ◆ ◆ ◆

Quahog (clam) chowder is one of the foods New England is known for worldwide. During the summer season, up and down the New England coast you'll find chowder contests where participants compete for the richest, most traditional, and tastiest chowder. We've won our share. If you want to make good chowder, you have to start with great clams. We've had this chowder on our menu since '71 ~ it has to be good!

2 ounces salt pork, rind removed
2 cups diced onion
1 cup diced celery
3 cups diced potatoes
1 teaspoon dried thyme
1 teaspoon ground black pepper

4 cups shelled quahogs with juice
  (about 6 pounds in shell)
$\frac{1}{2}$ cup salted butter
$\frac{1}{2}$ cup all-purpose flour
$1\frac{1}{2}$ quarts light cream

1. Dice the salt pork and sauté in a large pot until translucent.

2. Add the onions and celery and sauté for 5 minutes.

3. Pour in about $1\frac{1}{2}$ cups of the juice from the clams and add the potatoes and seasonings.

4. Simmer this mixture until the potatoes are tender. This should take about 10 minutes.

5. Melt the butter in a small saucepan. When it is bubbling, add the flour and cook for about 5 minutes, stirring often. This is called a roux, pronounced "rue."

6. Roughly chop the quahogs, reserving any liquid.

7. When the potatoes are tender, add the quahogs to the large pot and simmer for 2 minutes.

8. Stir in the roux and continue simmering for another 5 minutes, stirring frequently. This is your chowder base.

9. In a separate saucepan, scald the cream by heating it until small bubbles appear around the edges of the pan. Do not boil.

10. Stir the hot scalded cream into the chowder base, mix together, and remove from heat.

11. At The Black Dog, we serve it topped with a dollop of butter, accompanied by oyster crackers or crusty bread.

SERVES 8 TO 10

BLACK DOG TAVERN

Sorry but our chowder cups did not arrive, so we can't open until Monday, Jan. 11th.

From the Vineyard Gazette · January, 1971

Joshua Slocum's Fish Chowder
AS RENDERED IN SHENANDOAH'S GALLEY

◆ ◆ ◆ ◆ ◆

Joshua Slocum recorded this simple recipe, slightly modified by The Black Dog cooks, as he sailed alone around the world. It's one of Capt. Douglas's most frequently requested dishes, both on board and off. It's exceptionally creamy ~ we think it tastes great, but know it tastes best when simmered on a coal stove at sea while loafing down-wind.

1 large onion, chopped
¼ cup butter (or bacon fat)
5 large potatoes, cut in ½-inch cubes
4 cups light cream
1 cup fish stock (see page 43)
salt to taste
2 pounds fresh skinless and boneless cod fillets
1 teaspoon ground white pepper
1 teaspoon chopped fresh parsley
¼ teaspoon dried thyme
garnish: butter, paprika

1. Wilt the onion in butter until soft and clear.

2. Add the potatoes and cover with cream and stock. Add a
   pinch of salt. Heat gently until tender. If you don't have any
   fish stock available, just add more cream.

3. Cut the fish in 1-inch pieces and add the fish and seasonings.
   Simmer until the fish flakes easily. Be careful not to allow the
   soup to boil. Adjust seasoning.

4. Serve in mugs or bowls with a bit of butter floating on top.
   Sprinkle with paprika if you like.

SERVES 6

Smoked Bluefish & Corn Chowder

An end-of-season favorite, this chowder is made at the Tavern with native corn from Morning Glory Farm and Chappaquiddick Smoked Bluefish. How local can you get? Since you don't have access to our walk-in cooler, you could substitute your favorite smoked fish for the bluefish.

4 tablespoons salted butter
½ cup diced onion
½ cup diced celery
¼ cup all-purpose flour
6 cups hot chicken or fish stock
2 cups diced new potatoes
2 cups fresh corn kernels (about 4 ears)
¼ teaspoon thyme
½ teaspoon black pepper
½ pound shredded smoked bluefish
1 cup light cream

1. In a heavy-bottomed pot, melt the butter over medium low heat.

2. Add the onions and celery and sauté slowly, partially covered, until they are translucent.

3. Sprinkle the melted butter and veggies with the flour. Continue cooking and stirring over low heat for about 5 minutes. Let the flour and butter mixture bubble slowly until the flour has cooked but not browned.

4. Stir in the hot stock and bring to a boil. Add potatoes, fresh corn, and seasonings. Lower heat to a simmer and cook until the potatoes are soft.

5. Add the smoked bluefish and continue simmering for another two minutes. Remove from heat and stir in the cream.

SERVES 6 TO 8

◆ Vidalia Onion Soup ◆

◆ ◆ ◆ ◆ ◆

In early spring, when Georgia's Vidalia onions hit the market, they quickly appear on The Black Dog's menu. Their unique sweetness adds interest to many dishes. We often just slice them into ½-inch slabs, top with a little salt, pepper, and melted butter and grill them for 3 or 4 minutes. But on a cool summer night, there's nothing better than this soup.

2 tablespoons canola oil
4 large Vidalia onions, thinly slivered
    (may substitute Walla Walla, Maui, or other sweet onions)
½ cup dry sherry
1½ quarts chicken stock (see page 44)
2 teaspoons chopped fresh thyme
2 bay leaves
2 teaspoons salt
1 teaspoon ground white pepper
grated Parmigiano-Reggiano

1. Preheat a heavy-bottomed saucepan. Add the oil. When it starts smoking, stir in the onions.

2. Reduce the heat and allow the onions to brown evenly, caramelizing the natural sugars. This intensifies their sweetness and overall flavor. Don't let them burn.

3. Add the sherry and deglaze the pan, incorporating any browned bits of onion.

4. Pour in the stock, herbs, and seasonings. Stir together and bring to a boil.

5. Reduce to a simmer for about twenty minutes.

6. Serve with a sprinkling of grated cheese.

SERVES 6

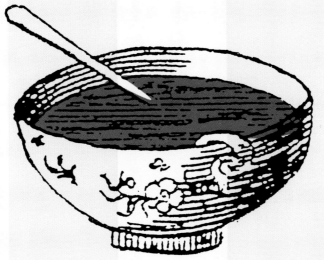

Watercress Mushroom Soup

◆ ◆ ◆ ◆ ◆

One of our favorite summer greens is watercress. It grows along the upper ends of some of the streambeds on the Island. One of the local farmers picks the cress for us a couple of times a week, depending on our needs, and the rate of growth (if the migrating ducks haven't found it first). The vibrant greens are generally served in a salad or as a garnish the first day. If we have any left, the next day it becomes soup or salad dressing. The peppery cress adds a nice touch to this quick and easy light chicken-based soup that is good on a rainy summer day.

2 tablespoons olive oil
½ cup diced onion
½ cup diced carrot
½ cup diced celery
1 cup sliced mushrooms
6 cups chicken stock,
    (see recipe, page 44)
1 cup diced cooked chicken
1 cup chopped watercress
¼ teaspoon dried basil or
    1 tablespoon chopped fresh basil
salt and pepper

1. Sauté the celery, carrot, mushrooms, and onion in the olive oil until tender.

2. Add the stock and bring to a boil.

3. Add the chicken, watercress, and basil and simmer for about five minutes.

4. Correct seasoning by adding salt and pepper if necessary.

5. Serve in steaming mugs.

SERVES 4 TO 6

◆ Tavern Gazpacho ◆

◆ ◆ ◆ ◆ ◆

There's a pace to life on the Island. We call it "Island time." Seems as though we're always waiting for something ~ like the next ferry to come in, or the fishing boats to arrive, or the local tomatoes to ripen. There's nothing quite like the first batch of radiant red ripe tomatoes. Soon after the bonanza begins, we help out Andrew Woodruff of Whippoorwill farm, our local grower, by buying some of the less picture-perfect but delicious tomatoes. We then make batches of gazpacho ~ a treat on hot summer days.

3 pounds tomatoes
1 small red onion
1 peeled and seeded
   cucumber
1 red pepper, seeded
4 scallions
2 stalks celery
1 quart tomato juice
½ cup red wine vinegar
½ cup olive oil
1 teaspoon Tabasco
¼ cup chopped fresh basil
2 teaspoons Worcestershire
   sauce
salt and pepper to taste
1 cup sour cream
garnish: 1 lime, cut in wedges

1. Finely dice all the veggies. You can chop them by hand or use a food processor if you watch it carefully. You don't want mush.

2. In a large bowl, blend the diced vegetables with the tomato juice, oil, vinegar, and seasonings.

3. Chill, covered, for several hours. (Or overnight for the best flavor.)

4. Serve in bowls with a dollop of sour cream and garnish with a wedge of fresh lime.

SERVES 6

◆

◆ Chilled Melon Soup ◆

◆ ◆ ◆ ◆ ◆

Serve this soup as a refreshing first course, or as a light lunch on a hot day. For best flavor, be sure that your melons are ripe. If the blossom end of the melon is very aromatic, that's generally a good sign.

1 ripe cantaloupe
½ ripe honeydew or crenshaw
½ pound red seedless grapes
2 ounces dry sherry
4 ounces fresh apple cider
½ teaspoon salt
1 tablespoon brown sugar
sour cream and fresh mint leaves for garnish

1. Cut melons in half and scoop out seeds into a fine holed strainer placed in a bowl. Push down on the seeds to extract all the juice. Reserve the juice.

2. Cut up melon flesh into chunks.

3. Place the melon juice, melon, and all the other ingredients, excluding the garnish, in a large blender or food processor and pulse until smooth. It may be easier to do this in 2 batches.

4. Strain mixture through a fine-holed sieve or food mill. Chill.

5. Serve cold, garnished with a dollop of sour cream and a bit of fresh mint.

SERVES 4

◆ Carrot Ginger Soup ◆

◆ ◆ ◆ ◆ ◆

If you love ginger, you'll love this soup. It has a bright, delicious fresh flavor that satisfies. As for the ginger, besides adding great flavor, it's been known to help quiet queasiness and that rocking and rolling feeling some of us get on the water.

¼ cup canola oil
1 cup chopped onion
¼ cup peeled and grated fresh ginger
4 cups chopped carrots, peeled
4 cups vegetable stock (see page 45)
2 tablespoons salt
1 tablespoon ground white pepper
2 teaspoons ground coriander
sliced scallions for garnish

1. Heat the oil in a large saucepan. Add the onion and ginger and sauté for 5 minutes.

2. Add all the remaining ingredients, except the scallions, and bring to a boil. Reduce to a simmer and continue cooking for about 15 minutes or until the carrots are soft.

3. Purée the hot mixture. Serve garnished with a few bits of chopped scallion.

SERVES 4

◆ Roasted Eggplant Soup ◆

◆ ◆ ◆ ◆ ◆

August abundance on the Island makes our winter dreams come true with eggplant, tomatoes, and fresh herbs ready for picking, or picking up, at the Farmer's Market in West Tisbury.

2 whole eggplants
½ cup olive oil
1 head elephant garlic
2 pounds fresh plum tomatoes
1 onion, diced
1 red pepper, diced
1 green pepper, diced
2 quarts vegetable stock or chicken stock
   (see pages 44 & 45)
3 tablespoons chopped fresh basil
3 tablespoons chopped fresh oregano
3 tablespoons chopped fresh parsley
2 cups ricotta
salt and pepper to taste

1. Preheat oven to 425°F.

2. Cut the eggplants in half. Drizzle with ¼ cup olive oil. Place on a baking sheet with the head of garlic and the whole tomatoes. Roast in the preheated oven for about 30 minutes or until soft.

3. When the vegetables are cool, remove any stem remains and skin from the eggplant and tomatoes. Coarsely chop, reserving any liquid.

4. Remove the pulp from the garlic by gently squeezing the skin. Set aside.

5. Heat remaining olive oil in a large saucepan, and sauté the diced onion and peppers until onion is transparent.

6. Add the stock, herbs, and chopped eggplant-tomato mixture to the saucepan.

7. Reduce to a simmer and continue cooking over a low flame. The soup should be ready in about thirty minutes.

8. While the soup is cooking, blend the garlic and ricotta in a food processor. Add salt and pepper to the mixture and set aside.

9. After thirty minutes, adjust the soup seasoning with salt and pepper. Serve with a dollop of the garlic-ricotta mixture on top.

SERVES 6

◆

◆ Split Pea Soup ◆

◆ ◆ ◆ ◆ ◆

Why split pea in the summer? On rainy days on Martha's Vineyard people don't go to the beach, they go shopping and out to eat. We serve more soup on one of those rainy days than we do in a week in winter. The chowder pipeline is always open, and we usually make a huge pot of split pea ~ comfort food.

1 pound (2 cups) dried split peas
6 cups water or chicken stock (see page 44)
1 pound ham hock (optional)
1 tablespoon dry mustard
1/2 teaspoon dried thyme
1/2 teaspoon dried rosemary
1 teaspoon dried basil
1 pinch of ground cloves
1 teaspoon salt

2 1/2 tablespoons olive oil
4 cloves garlic, minced
1 cup diced onion
1 cup diced carrot
1 cup diced celery
1/2 cup diced red bell pepper
1 cup dark beer
1 to 2 tablespoons tamari or soy sauce

1. Rinse the split peas in a colander and then transfer them to a large stockpot along with 6 cups of water or stock.

2. Bring this to a boil and reduce to a simmer, stir, and skim off the foam as it develops.

3. When the peas have stopped foaming add the seasonings. Add the ham hock, if desired.

4. Cook at a low simmer for two hours, partially covered, making sure that the liquid doesn't completely evaporate. Have a little water or stock on hand to add, just in case.

5. Heat the olive oil in a large saucepan and sauté the onion, carrot, celery, red pepper and garlic until the onion is translucent.

6. Now remove the ham hock, if you have used one, from the pot and set aside to cool.

7. Stir the sautéed garlic and vegetables into the pot and add the beer. Cook for another half-hour.

8. Trim the meat off the hock and chop into bitesize pieces. Add it to the soup. Taste, add the tamari and whisk the soup. Correct the seasoning if necessary.

SERVES 8 TO 10

◆

♦ Hot & Sour Soup ♦

♦ ♦ ♦ ♦

Sometimes the best relief on a hot summer day comes from a bowl of hot, spicy soup. Many examples of this can be found in Asian cuisines. With typical Yankee practicality, we've adopted and adapted this old standby. The "hot" comes from the white pepper, not the chilis, and combined with the sour vinegar, it will cool you off and clear your sinuses. This recipe works equally well with sautéed pork strips or grilled fresh tuna. Luckily now most groceries stock what used to be "exotic" ingredients.

12 dried shiitake mushrooms
2 ounces dried lily buds*
10 dried tree ears*
1 cup fresh button mushrooms
3/4 pound lean pork loin
   or fresh tuna
4 tablespoons vegetable oil
1 tablespoon dark sesame oil
7 scallions, sliced

1 teaspoon white pepper
   or more to taste
1/2 cup kim chee* ~ optional
8 cups rich chicken stock (see page 44)
1/2 cup cider vinegar
6 tablespoons tamari
1/2 pound fresh tofu
2 beaten eggs
*available at specialty markets

1. Soak the dried shiitakes, lily buds, and tree ears, each in two cups of hot water in their own separate bowls. Let them soak for twenty minutes.

2. Slice the refreshed shiitake mushrooms while reserving the soaking liquid. Drain the lily buds and tree ears and rinse. Tear the tree ears into smaller pieces and remove any hard parts.

3. Slice the fresh mushrooms and set aside. Slice the pork or tuna in thin strips.

4. Place a large saucepan or large wok over high heat. Add the vegetable oil and sesame oil. Sauté the pork and scallions. When the pork loses its pinkness, add the fresh mushrooms.

5. Now add the shiitake mushrooms, tree ears, and lily buds, and cook to heat through. This should take about two minutes.

6. Season with the white pepper. Add the kim chee if you like.

7. Add the mushroom soaking liquid and the chicken stock. Stir to blend and add the vinegar and tamari. Bring the mixture to a boil, lower to a simmer, and taste.

8. Adjust the hot and sour balance by adding additional pepper or vinegar, carefully.

9. Slice the tofu into strips and add to soup.

10. Turn off the heat and stir in the beaten eggs.

SERVES 8 TO 10 ♦

A LL OF The Black Dog's salad dressings are made from scratch. What we offer on a daily basis depends on what fresh ingredients are available and the cook's preference. We typically start with a basic vinaigrette, and add fresh herbs and other ingredients. Most of our recipes are three to four parts oil to one part acid ~ depending on how tangy a taste is desired. It's so easy to whisk together oil, vinegar, a little salt and pepper, and a bit of Dijon mustard or fresh herbs ~ why ever buy bottled dressing? When you make it yourself, you know what you're eating.

Tamato
Basil
vinaigrette

LEMON
VINAIGR

Roasted
PEPPER
VINAIGRETTE

~ LEMON ~
esame Soy

◆ Salads ◆

Fresh Basil Vinaigrette

◆ ◆ ◆ ◆ ◆

A dressing for all reasons ~ nothing says summer like fresh basil. This mixture tastes great drizzled over sliced beefsteak tomatoes or steamed asparagus, as well as tossed with fresh greens. You can also use it to marinate chicken or fish. Make sure to use young, tender basil leaves.

2 small cloves garlic
$^{1}/_{2}$ teaspoon salt
$^{1}/_{2}$ to $^{3}/_{4}$ cup fresh basil leaves,
   loosely packed
$^{1}/_{4}$ cup extra virgin olive oil
$^{1}/_{4}$ cup canola oil
$^{1}/_{8}$ cup red wine vinegar
2 teaspoons Dijon mustard
$^{1}/_{4}$ teaspoon fresh ground pepper

1. Put the salt and garlic in a food processor or blender and pulse to chop and combine.
2. Now add the remainder of the ingredients and continue pulsing until the basil is minced and the vinaigrette is well combined.

YIELDS: 1 CUP

Lemon Sesame Soy Dressing

◆ ◆ ◆ ◆ ◆

If you are a sesame fan, you'll enjoy this dressing. Great on shredded carrot salad, it also works well as a marinade for lamb or swordfish. It will hold in the refrigerator for several days.

$^{1}/_{3}$ cup fresh lemon juice
$^{1}/_{2}$ cup soy sauce
$^{3}/_{4}$ cup canola oil
$^{1}/_{4}$ cup sesame oil
1 bunch scallions, thinly sliced
$^{1}/_{3}$ cup toasted sesame seeds

Whisk together all the ingredients in a small bowl or place in a jar and shake!

YIELDS: 2 CUPS

LEMON SESAME SOY
S·A·L·A·D
DRESSING

Sun~Dried Tomato Vinaigrette

◆ ◆ ◆ ◆ ◆

Another multi-purpose dressing, this richly flavored vinaigrette works well with any salad combination ~ fresh greens or chilled pasta. Try it with grilled shrimp.

¼ cup sun-dried tomatoes
¼ cup warm water
2 teaspoons Dijon-style mustard
1 clove garlic
3 large fresh basil leaves
¼ cup red wine vinegar
½ cup extra virgin olive oil
salt and pepper to taste

1. If you are using sun-dried tomatoes packed in oil, skip this step. Soak dry tomatoes in the warm water until soft. This should take about 20 minutes. When the tomato slices are soft, squeeze any excess liquid from the tomatoes and discard the soaking water.

2. Place the tomatoes in a blender or food processor and add the mustard, garlic, basil and vinegar. Blend together.

3. With the processor on, add the olive oil in a slow but steady stream. (If you have used tomatoes packed in oil, decrease the amount of olive oil.) The dressing should be on the thick side.

4. Add salt and pepper to taste.

YIELDS: 1¾ CUPS

◆

Roasted Red Pepper Vinaigrette

◆ ◆ ◆ ◆ ◆

Sweet, smoky roasted peppers are a favorite addition to many dishes. Use this dressing over field greens, add a few fresh pepper strips for extra crunch, and enjoy a delightful combination of flavors.

1 large or 2 medium red bell peppers
2 cloves garlic
2 tablespoons Dijon mustard
¼ cup red wine vinegar
1 cup extra virgin olive oil
salt and pepper

1. Roast the red pepper under a broiler, turning frequently to achieve an evenly charred skin, or spear with a large fork and hold over a gas flame until evenly charred. Place charred pepper in a paper bag and close tightly. Let it sit in the bag for at least 10 minutes. Remove from the bag and the charred skin should easily peel off. Cut open and remove the seeds.

2. Put the pepper, garlic, mustard, and vinegar into a food processor or a blender and pulse until smooth.

3. Slowly pour in the olive oil, maintaining a steady stream, until the vinaigrette is smooth and well blended.

4. Add salt and pepper to taste.

YIELDS: 1½ CUPS

◆

Beet, Orange & Feta Salad

◆ ◆ ◆ ◆ ◆

Refreshing and colorful, this lightly dressed salad is a perfect accompaniment to grilled lamb and is equally tasty on its own.

¼ cup extra virgin olive oil
2 tablespoons balsamic vinegar
1 sprig fresh rosemary
8 ounces feta cheese, cut into ½-inch cubes

3 medium-size beets
2 seedless oranges
8 ounces mixed salad greens

1. Chill four salad plates.

2. Place olive oil, vinegar, the leaves of the rosemary, and feta cubes into a small bowl. Toss together and set aside, covered.

3. Boil beets covered in water for a half hour. Drain and cool. Peel and cut into ¼-inch slices.

4. Peel and segment the oranges, removing all the white membranes.

5. To assemble the salads, take four chilled salad plates and cover each with tossed mixed greens. Top the greens with beets, orange segments, and seasoned feta dressing.

SERVES 4

◆ Watercress Mushroom Salad ◆

◆ ◆ ◆ ◆ ◆

One of the favorite greens at **The Black Dog** is watercress. We prize it for its unique peppery taste, and because we are lucky enough to have an ample supply of just-picked greens. There are places on the Island where it grows abundantly. This easy salad is a great combination of contrasting textures and summer flavors.

2 bunches watercress
1 cup fresh mixed mushrooms, cleaned and sliced
12 calamata olives
2 tablespoons fresh grated Parmigiano-Reggiano
1 cup Fresh Basil Vinaigrette, see page 63

1. Pick through the watercress and discard any wilted or bruised leaves. Cut off the stems, wash and dry thoroughly.

2. Divide the watercress among 4 chilled plates and add the mushrooms. Garnish with olives and cheese and serve the dressing on the side.

SERVES 4

*A*LL OF THE PEN-AND-INK "how to" illustrations in this

book were created by Charlie (a/k/a Char-lee) Esposito shown

with tools in hand. The Black Dog's "Renaissance Man,"

Charlie's been on the crew since the early '70s, cooking Chinese Night, running the floor,

and in his off-hours, operating a recording studio. We thought his photo belonged in the

"squid section" since it seems to be his favorite word (and dish). He uses it for nearly

everything, from his email code to his record label ~ "Squid Rocket Records."

How to Clean Squid

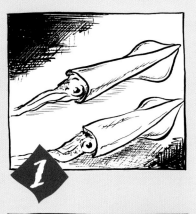
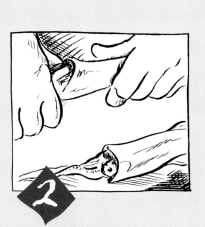

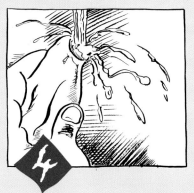

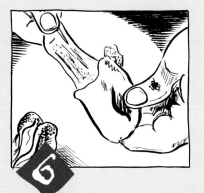
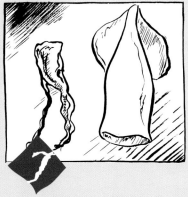

1 The whole fresh squid.

2 While holding the squid body, pull the head off. The innards and clear cartilage should come out with it.

3 Pull the remaining innards out with your fingers.

4 Rinse the squid body inside and out with cold water and set aside.

5 While holding the head, cut the tentacles off in one piece. Feel for the hard beak and discard if present.

6 Peel the skin from the body.

7 The cleaned squid with the body whole.

8 Slice the squid body into rings. They are ready to use.

◆ Fresh Squid Salad ◆

◆ ◆ ◆ ◆ ◆

With a little planning and quick preparation, you can enjoy this tasty salad on a hot summer day.

½ cup extra virgin olive oil
¼ cup fresh squeezed lemon juice
3 cloves garlic, chopped
1 tablespoon chopped fresh oregano
½ tablespoon chopped fresh basil
1 teaspoon salt
½ teaspoon ground white pepper
¼ teaspoon crushed red pepper
1 red onion, thinly sliced

½ green pepper cut in thin strips
½ sweet red pepper cut in thin strips
4 scallions, cut into one-inch strips
1 medium cucumber, peeled, cut in half
    lengthwise, seeded, and sliced crosswise
    into thin crescents
1 pound cleaned squid, rings and tentacles
    (See "How to Clean Squid" on page 69)
fresh mixed greens

1. Pour half the olive oil and all the lemon juice into a medium-size mixing bowl. Add the garlic, chopped herbs, and other seasonings, and stir. Add the thinly sliced vegetables and toss gently. Set aside.

2. Heat a heavy skillet over high heat and pour in the remaining olive oil. When the oil starts to smoke, toss the squid into the pan and sauté for two minutes. Remove from heat and drain.

3. Stir the squid into vegetable mixture and chill for two hours, covered.

4. Serve over a bed of fresh greens.

SERVES 4

Where's the Oven Stretcher?

As you probably guessed, **The Black Dog** has never been without a practical joker in the kitchen. New members of our dishwashing crew, the unsung heroes of every restaurant, are quickly exposed to the kitchen's humor and wind up on scavenger hunts for very specialized imaginary equipment. We can generally spot the "new guy" easily because he's still trying to find the "oven stretcher" ~ a tool guaranteed to push an oven's walls out into another dimension.

✦ Swordfish en Escabeche ✦

✦✦✦✦✦

Try this Black Dog specialty, a tribute to the Menemsha Harbor swordfishing fleet, as an easy and dramatic appetizer. It can also be served over fresh greens as a first course salad. Escabeche is a spicy pickling marinade, popular in Spain. At The Black Dog we use odd cuts of swordfish, also called nubs. Ask your fishmonger for these odds and ends, which should be less expensive than swordfish steaks. Thanks to aggressive intervention and quota restrictions, overfishing of swordfish has been halted and these prize fish are available again for all of us to enjoy.

1 cup extra-virgin olive oil
1½ pounds fresh swordfish odd cuts, cut into 1¼-inch cubes
1 large Spanish onion cut in 1½-inch pieces
1 each green, red, and yellow bell pepper cut into 1½-inch squares
1 garlic clove, chopped
¾ cup red wine vinegar
½ to 1 tablespoon salt
1 teaspoon ground black pepper
1 tablespoon fresh oregano, roughly chopped
1 tablespoon orange zest, julienne
dash crushed red pepper
2 tablespoons capers, drained and rinsed
fresh greens

1. Heat half the oil in a heavy-bottomed skillet and brown the swordfish nubs, turning carefully with tongs until tender (about 5 minutes).

2. Remove browned pieces individually and place in mixing bowl. Reserve.

3. Discard the cooking oil.

4. Heat the remaining oil in the same skillet. Add the onion and sauté for two minutes, then add peppers and garlic and continue cooking for about 3 more minutes, stirring occasionally.

5. Pour in vinegar and add the seasonings. Cook for 5 more minutes. Adjust salt.

6. Pour over swordfish. Sprinkle capers on top and chill covered, for at least four hours.

7. Serve over fresh greens.

SERVES 4 TO 6

*T*HE COASTWISE Packet building sits on the beach right next to **The Black Dog**. Its dock runs in front of the Tavern and can be a bustling place in the summer. Often it's crowded with a combination of folks ~ some waiting for a meal at the Tavern and others ready to sail on *Shenandoah* or *Alabama*. Running the sailing operation is a busy family affair but occasionally there's time when we can cajole Charlene Douglas to model for **The Black Dog Catalog** ~ here she is smiling with Magnolia and Rosebud ~ both cherished four-legged members of her family.

◆ Black Bean & Sirloin Tip Salad ◆

◆ ◆ ◆ ◆ ◆

One of the best things about summer food is the abundance and variety of fresh greens and the rich, sweet taste of vine ripened tomatoes, but grazing on salad greens won't satisfy most of us. Here's a recipe that combines summer bounty with flavorful, healthy eating. It relies on black beans to supply protein and nutrients and uses steak as a condiment rather than the main course. For the carnivores among us, add as much or as little sirloin as you like.

1 cup black beans
2 quarts water
1 tablespoon Dijon mustard
1/3 cup fresh lemon juice
1 teaspoon chili powder
1 teaspoon ground cumin
1/4 cup olive oil

1/2 medium red onion, diced
1/2 bunch scallions, chopped
salt and fresh ground pepper to taste
1 to 1 1/2 pounds grilled sirloin tips

4 cups mixed field greens
1 cup chopped vine-ripened tomatoes

TO PREPARE THE BEANS
(Best if done a day ahead)

1. First spread the dry beans out in a shallow roasting pan and pick through them carefully. You want to remove any small stones, bits of clay, or other non-food material.

2. Put the beans in a sieve and rinse them under running water for 1 or 2 minutes.

3. Place the rinsed beans in a medium bowl with enough water to cover them, and soak for a few hours or overnight.

4. After soaking, drain, and rinse again.

5. Place the beans in a pot with two quarts of water and bring to a boil. Reduce heat and then simmer gently, stirring occasionally, until tender. This should take about 90 minutes or less.

6. Drain and refrigerate for later use. You should have about 2 1/2 cups of cooked beans.

TO ASSEMBLE THE SALAD

1. In a large bowl, mix together the mustard, lemon juice, seasoning, olive oil, red onion, and scallions. Add the beans and toss to season well. Refrigerate for a least one hour.

2. Grill sirloin tips to your preferred level of doneness. For this salad, we think medium rare is best. Slice into strips.

3. Place a handful of field greens on each plate and top with a generous amount of the chilled black bean mixture. Lay a few strips of sliced sirloin over the beans and top the steak with chopped tomatoes.

SERVES 4 TO 6

◆

◆ Curried Chicken Salad ◆

◆ ◆ ◆ ◆ ◆

How do you slice a grape? With a smile of expectation when you are making this elegant salad, ideal for entertaining. We serve it often at catered affairs. The recipe will serve eight, or you can enjoy leftovers.

CHICKEN

3 cups cooked chicken

Either poach a three-pound chicken, cool, and remove meat ~ or use leftover cooked chicken. Dice into ½-inch pieces. Reserve.

CURRY DRESSING

2 egg yolks	2 scallions
1 tablespoon curry powder	5 basil leaves
1 tablespoon lemon juice	1 cup canola oil
1 small clove garlic, chopped	½ cup mango chutney
¼ teaspoon chopped fresh ginger	½ cup heavy cream
1 teaspoon salt	

1. In a food processor, beat the egg yolks. Then add the curry powder, lemon juice, chopped garlic, ginger, salt, scallions and basil leaves. Pulse to blend.

2. While the processor is running, slowly pour the oil into the mixture. It should emulsify.

3. Remove the mixture from the processor to a large bowl. Add the chutney and heavy cream. Mix well.

TO PREPARE SALAD

2 scallions, sliced
½ red pepper, seeded and diced
½ apple, diced
¼ pound red seedless grapes, sliced in half
2 stalks celery, chopped
5 basil leaves, chopped in strips
½ cup water chestnuts, chopped

1. Combine the diced chicken, scallions, red pepper, apples, grapes, celery, basil and water chestnuts. Toss together and season with dressing.

2. Serve on your favorite greens.

SERVES 6 TO 8

◆

◆ Nancy Oh's Pickled Vegetables ◆

◆ ◆ ◆ ◆ ◆

For more than ten years, Nancy Oh has been the backbone of our kitchen prep crew. During the late 1980's, Nancy immigrated with her husband Kevin from Malaysia, and along with their extended family, they were affectionately dubbed "Oh and the Oh-ettes" by the crew. Kevin and Nancy have contributed a great deal to our menu. Here's one of our favorite veggie combinations. It should be refrigerated for two days to meld the flavors before serving, so plan ahead. You can use it to add zip to a cold sandwich plate or serve it with grilled meat or fish. It will keep in the refrigerator far longer than you can restrain yourself from finishing it off.

1 medium carrot, peeled
1 small red bell pepper, seeded
1 cucumber, peeled and seeded
1 poblano pepper, seeded
½ Daikon radish, peeled
½ cup jicama, peeled
½ cup green cabbage

½ cup bok choy
3-inch piece of fresh ginger,
    peeled and cut in thin slivers
3 tablespoons salt
1 cup sugar
1 cup white vinegar

1. Two days before serving, cut all the veggies (except the ginger) to a matchstick size or julienne. The goal is ¼ x ¼ by 2-inches. (Be careful when you seed and chop the hot pepper, and keep your hands away from your face ~ the oil from it can burn your eyes.)

2. In a large bowl, sprinkle the veggies with the salt and toss to coat them thoroughly. Place the salted veggies in a colander or large strainer and let them stand and drain at room temperature for about 3 hours.

3. Rinse the veggies, and place in a large glass container. Add the sugar, ginger, and the vinegar. Mix well.

4. Cover and refrigerate for a minimum of 2 days before using. Stir thoroughly after the first day.

YIELDS: 5 CUPS

◆ Moroccan Cous Cous ◆

◆ ◆ ◆ ◆ ◆

Whether you serve our colorful version of this tasty African grain as a side dish with grilled meat, or as a flavorful salad for a cool lunch, the reaction will be "delicious!"

1 medium tomato
1 small red onion
1 red bell pepper
½ bunch scallions
¼ cup lemon juice
1 clove garlic, chopped
½ cup extra virgin olive oil
1 teaspoon salt
½ teaspoon ground cumin
½ teaspoon cayenne pepper (optional)
1 tablespoon fresh chopped parsley
   (you may substitute cilantro, basil,
   or mint ~ your choice)
2 cups cooked cous cous (see below)

1. Chop the vegetables into a small dice, about ¼-inch.

2. In a large bowl, combine the vegetables, the lemon juice, the garlic, and ¼ cup of the olive oil, reserving the remainder. Toss together and add the seasonings.

3. Add the cooked, fluffed cous cous to the bowl, incorporating it into the veggie mixture.

4. Now add the remaining oil in small increments until the cous cous mixture is moist and no large clumps remain.

5. Chill for at least three hours or overnight to allow the flavors to meld.

TO COOK COUS COUS
1 cup Moroccan cous cous
1 cup boiling water
2 teaspoons salt

1. Pour the boiling water in a medium bowl. Add the salt and let it dissolve.

2. Add the cous cous. Mix well and cover for about five to eight minutes.

3. Fluff with a fork. Reserve.

SERVES 4 TO 6 AS A SIDE DISH, 2 FOR LUNCH

Roasted Eggplant & Pepper Salad

❖ ❖ ❖ ❖ ❖

You'll enjoy the next-best-thing to August veggies from the West Tisbury Farmer's Market when you make this chilled salad. You just have to rough chop this earthy mix and then kick back while it bakes.

2 large eggplants
1 large red bell pepper
1 large green bell pepper
2 stalks celery
2 tablespoons fresh basil
1 tablespoon fresh oregano
1 head garlic
1 large Spanish or Vidalia onion

1 small fennel bulb
1/2 cup extra virgin olive oil
1 cup balsamic vinegar
1/2 cup brown sugar
1 tablespoon Tabasco
1 teaspoon salt
1/2 teaspoon fresh ground black pepper
mixed field greens or tender spinach leaves

1. Preheat the oven to 425°F.

2. Cut the eggplants into approximately 2-inch cubes (larger rather than smaller). Seed, core, and cut the peppers in wide strips.

3. Coarsely chop the celery, basil, and oregano. Peel the garlic cloves and leave them whole. Slice the onion into generous pieces, about 1/4-inch. The fennel bulb should be sliced thin. Toss all the prepared veggies into a large roasting pan.

4. In a small bowl, mix together the olive oil, vinegar, brown sugar, Tabasco, salt and pepper.

5. Pour this mixture over the veggies and toss to coat well.

6. Cover the roasting pan with foil and bake for about 45 minutes.

7. After baking, chill the mixture for about 2 hours.

8. Serve on your favorite greens.

SERVES 8

How to Chop Garlic

1 Separate the individual cloves from the bulb.

2 Push down with the side of a knife blade to smash slightly and break the skin of the clove.

3 Peel the parchment-like skins off the garlic and push aside.

4 Hold clove steady with your fingers pressing downward.

5 Start slicing the individual peeled cloves.

6 Continue to slice all the peeled cloves.

7 Dice the sliced cloves.

8 Mince garlic as fine as needed. Sometimes a coarsely minced or sliced clove is all that's needed.

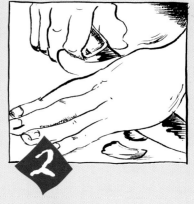
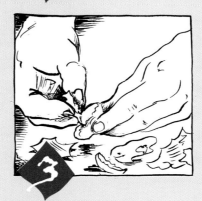
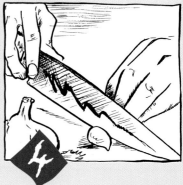

Pasta

Angelhair Pasta with Shrimp & Feta Cheese

◆ ◆ ◆ ◆ ◆

This is a quick summer dish that has been on our menu for years. It's best in August when the tomatoes are ripe and have the most flavor, although most grocery stores have vine-ripened tomatoes year 'round. If the shrimp are prepped ahead of time, you can throw this dish together in about twenty minutes.

3 to 5 cloves of garlic, chopped
3 tablespoons olive oil
1 pound small shrimp, peeled and
    deveined (see page 96)
¼ cup dry white wine
4 ripe tomatoes, diced

small bunch of fresh basil leaves
1 tablespoon salt
8 ounces feta cheese, crumbled
1½ pounds of angelhair pasta
    (two 12-ounce packages)
salt and pepper to taste

1. Bring six quarts of water to a boil on high heat.

2. Sauté garlic in the olive oil over high heat until fragrant. Add shrimp and sauté briefly, just until the shrimp are pink.

3. Add the wine and let cook down briefly. Add the diced tomatoes, and lower the heat.

4. Tear the basil leaves into the sauce and add the feta cheese. Add fresh ground black pepper and salt to taste. Be careful not to overcook because shrimp will become rubbery. Set aside.

5. When pasta water comes to a rolling boil, add one tablespoon of salt and the angelhair pasta. The pasta will take about three minutes to cook, so time the sauce accordingly.

6. Drain the angelhair pasta quickly leaving a bit of the water and return to its pot. Add a bit of the sauce to moisten the pasta and divide among serving plates. Add the rest of the sauce to each plate and serve.

SERVES 6

◆ Char~lee's Chilled Spicy ◆
Sesame Noodles

◆ ◆ ◆ ◆ ◆

First introduced during one of our special Chinese nights during the winter, this recipe quickly became a fixture on our summer menu. It is probably Charlie's (a/k/a Char-lee's) most requested recipe ~ people stop him on the street and walk away with ingredients jotted on a scrap of paper. It makes nearly a quart of sauce and you'll be glad for the volume, because it keeps at least two weeks refrigerated and improves with age. You can use the sauce on stir-fried veggies or for a quick snack on cold noodles. You can also cut the recipe in half or double it easily.

1 pound fresh or dried egg noodles
1 cup tahini (tahini tends to separate;
  mix before measuring)
1 cup hot water
1 cup canola oil
1 cup tamari or soy sauce
½ cup sugar
½ cup vinegar (cider and/or red wine)
¼ to ½ cup chili oil
  (depending on how hot you want it)

2 tablespoons dark sesame oil
5 cloves garlic, peeled and chopped
3 scallions, chopped (for garnish)
Optional:
1 cucumber, peeled, seeded and sliced
1 grilled, sliced boneless chicken breast
2 tablespoons sesame seeds

1. Cook egg noodles in six quarts of boiling, salted water for about 3 to 5 minutes for fresh or 7 to 10 minutes for dried. Drain and rinse in cold water. Add a drizzle of sesame oil to prevent sticking. Chill.

2. Pour the cup of tahini into a large mixing bowl. Add the cup of hot water to the measuring cup, stir to clear any tahini left in the cup, and add to the bowl. Blend with a wire whisk until smooth.

3. Whisk in the vegetable oil to blend. Add the tamari, sugar, and vinegar, one at a time, blending with the whisk after each addition.

4. Add the chili oil starting with ¼ cup. Taste for spiciness. Add more if you like.

5. Add the sesame oil and garlic. Blend.

6. Divide the chilled noodles among four plates. Add enough sauce to coat, and garnish with chopped scallions and any optional ingredients. Enjoy! (Don't forget to refrigerate the remaining sauce.)

SERVES 4 AS A MAIN COURSE
OR 6 AS AN APPETIZER

Linguine with White Clam Sauce

❖ ❖ ❖ ❖

More than a classic ~ just taste our version and you'll see why it will always be on **The Black Dog** menu! If you decide to add the chilis, be sure to wash your hands after mincing them ~ any contact with your eyes should be avoided.

28 littleneck clams, scrubbed
7 cloves garlic, minced
2 tablespoons extra virgin olive oil
2 small hot chilis, minced (a tasty option)
½ cup dry white wine
freshly ground black pepper to taste

½ cup chopped fresh parsley
¼ cup chopped fresh basil
1 to 1½ pounds linguine
1 tablespoon salt

1. Bring six quarts of water to a rolling boil and add 1 tablespoon salt.

2. Open 24 of the clams over a bowl with a sieve to strain the clam liquid. Save 4 clams for garnish. Set the strained liquid aside and chop the clams to a mince.

3. Add the linguine to boiling water. The clam sauce should take the same length of time to cook as the linguine.

4. Sauté minced garlic in the olive oil over high heat, being careful not to burn it. Add the minced chilis if you like a spicy sauce.

5. Add the minced clams and sauté to heat through, then add the black pepper and white wine. Now add the reserved clam liquid.

6. Open the last four clams without detaching the clams from their shells, and toss them into the sauce. (Opening them helps the clams to cook quickly. See "How to Open Clams" on page 118.)

7. Add the parsley and basil. Lower the heat to medium.

8. When the linguine is al dente, drain it and toss it with about half of the sauce.

9. Divide the pasta onto four plates, add the remaining sauce, and garnish each plate with one of the whole clams.

SERVES 4

◆ Ravioli Pomadoro ◆

◆ ◆ ◆ ◆ ◆

This dish celebrates our native American tomato as the golden fruit ~ not in color, but in its value to so many dishes. If vine-ripened tomatoes are not available, use canned roma tomatoes for the best flavor.

1/2 tablespoon salt for pasta water
2 tablespoons virgin olive oil
1/4 to 1/2 teaspoon crushed red pepper
2 garlic cloves, chopped
1 medium red onion, chopped
4 to 6 large fresh tomatoes, chopped
10 to 12 fresh basil leaves, cut in strips
salt and pepper to taste
1 cup sliced white mushrooms

1 pound of your favorite fresh ravioli or pasta
grated Parmigiano-Reggiano
fresh basil for garnish

1. Bring 4 quarts of water to a boil and add salt.

2. Combine the olive oil and crushed red pepper in a large sauté pan and heat until smokin' hot.

3. Add the garlic and onions to the hot oil and sauté until translucent. Add the tomatoes and basil. Add salt and pepper to taste.

4. Continue cooking until the mixture is reduced by half.

5. Add the mushrooms to the tomato mixture and continue cooking for about three minutes. Now is the time to add ravioli or pasta to the boiling water, since fresh pasta usually cooks in about three minutes.

6. Drain pasta and top with the sauce. Garnish each serving with grated Parmigiano-Reggiano and fresh basil.

SERVES 4

◆

◆ Penne with ◆ Shiitake Mushroom Sauce

◆ ◆ ◆ ◆ ◆

We always start with the freshest and the best ~ the real secret to great food. Island-grown tomatoes have always been easy to come by, but mushrooms? That's where Matt Dix and Rebecca Miller's endeavors helped enrich our menu. Since 1994, we've had the luxury of locally grown shiitake mushrooms. At North Tabor Farm, in a shady spot on the north side of the Island, Matt and Rebecca have created a natural habitat for the shiitake to thrive. Using oak logs from the State Forest and shiitake spores, their mushrooms grow up to 3 inches in diameter. Rebecca, who spent her summer vacations during college working at The Black Dog, proudly states "Our shiitake grown on logs in a natural environment are much bigger and richer than the supermarket kind, and really meaty. They are wonderful." We agree!

½ ounce dried shiitake mushrooms
1 cup hot water
½ pound fresh shiitake mushroom caps
1 large portobello mushroom
1 pound fresh plum tomatoes
1 pound penne
1 tablespoon salt

6 tablespoons extra virgin olive oil
5 minced garlic cloves
ground black pepper to taste
1 cup white wine
10 basil leaves
½ teaspoon salt
grated Romano cheese

1. Pour one cup of hot water into a small bowl. Add the dried shiitake mushrooms and set aside to soak and rehydrate for about ten minutes.

2. Slice the fresh shiitakes and fresh portobello. When the dried shiitakes are soft, squeeze out any excess water. Reserve all the soaking liquid. Slice the soft shiitakes. Dice the tomatoes into large cubes.

3. Bring six quarts of water to a boil. Add 1 tablespoon of salt and the penne. Cook for approximately 10 minutes, until al dente.

4. While pasta is cooking, heat the olive oil in a heavy saucepan or deep cast iron skillet. Add the garlic and black pepper. Stir to keep the garlic from burning.

5. Add the sliced fresh mushrooms to the pan and stir to coat with the oil. Now add the softened shiitake slices and diced tomatoes.

6. Pour in white wine, stir for a minute, and then add the reserved mushroom soaking liquid.

7. Tear the basil leaves and stir into the pan. Add ½ teaspoon salt and bring the heat down to a low simmer. Continue cooking for about three to five minutes.

8. Serve penne with mushroom sauce and grated cheese.

SERVES 4

◆

◆ Linguine with Pesto ◆

❖❖❖❖❖

August is the time for basil ~ and that means pesto. Most summer afternoons at The Black Dog you can find Nancy Oh picking through a bushel or two of fresh basil from Whippoorwill Farm, carefully removing the leaves from the stems. Pesto making is a snap with a blender or food processor; you can have the sauce ready in minutes. If you have the time on a lazy summer afternoon try making it old-world style with a mortar and pestle. It may take longer, but the texture will be closer to its Genovese origins and the taste will be sweeter, since the oils from the basil, pinenuts, and garlic blend more slowly. Make sure to use the smaller tender basil leaves and save the larger ones for tomato sauces or roasting new potatoes. Add a diced vine-ripened tomato at the end, either directly onto the pasta or blended into the pesto. The acid from the tomato will cut some of the oiliness of the sauce. If you're not going to serve it right away, wait to add the cheese. Make a large batch and freeze it in serving-size containers. You add the cheese when you're ready to enjoy your pesto for a taste of hot summer days in January. Pesto is great as a substitute for tomato sauce on pizza ~ use fresh beefsteak tomato slices as a topping. It's also good served over grilled bluefish fillets.

2 tablespoons pinenuts
1 cup extra virgin olive oil
5 to 7 cloves garlic
3 cups fresh basil leaves
½ teaspoon sea salt
ground pepper to taste

3 tablespoons Parmigiano-Reggiano
1 ripe tomato (optional)
1 pound linguine
1 tablespoon salt

1. Toast the pinenuts over high heat in a dry skillet. Keep the pan and the pinenuts moving so they don't burn. This should take a minute or two.

2. Preheat your oven to 425°F. Drizzle a little olive oil on the unpeeled garlic cloves and roast until soft, about five minutes. This gives the garlic a sweeter, less biting taste.

3. Peel the garlic and add to a food processor or blender along with the toasted pinenuts and a little of the olive oil. Process briefly to a coarse texture.

4. Add a third of the basil leaves and a third of the olive oil and process on a slow setting. Continue this until all the basil and olive oil has been added. Add sea salt and pepper.

5. If you're serving the pesto soon, add the cheese and the optional ripe tomato.

6. Bring six quarts of water to a rolling boil and add 1 tablespoon of salt. Add the linguine, cook for about 10 minutes, until al dente. Drain and toss the cooked linguine with a little of the pesto. Divide onto plates and add the rest of the pesto on top. You can add more grated cheese, as desired.

SERVES 4

◆

◆ Penne Sautéed with ◆ Broccoli Rabe & White Beans

◆ ◆ ◆ ◆ ◆

In years past, broccoli rabe was only available in late spring and early fall. Now you can find it year 'round in most areas. It has a bite ~ slightly bitter ~ that we love, and adds dimension to this tasty vegetarian combo. If you've never tasted it before, try it before you make this dish. It's not to everyone's taste.

1 pound cannellini	1 tablespoon of salt
(a/k/a white kidney beans)	2 tablespoons olive oil
1 bunch broccoli rabe	1 tablespoon chopped garlic
1 tablespoon salt	salt and pepper to taste
1 pound penne	Parmigiano-Reggiano

1. The day before you plan to serve, soak the pound of beans overnight in four times their volume of water. Drain.

2. To cook, cover the beans in fresh water and bring to a boil. Reduce the heat to maintain a simmer, and cook until the beans are tender but still slightly firm. This should take about 30 to 40 minutes. Remove from heat and chill the beans in their cooking liquid.

3. Trim off the tough fibrous ends of the rabe and discard. Bring two quarts of water to a boil. Add a tablespoon of salt.

4. Place the rabe in the boiling water and stir. When the water comes back to a second boil, remove the rabe and plunge it into ice water to stop the cooking process. Reserve.

5. Bring 6 quarts of water to a boil, add 1 tablespoon of salt and the pound of penne. Cook approximately 7 to 9 minutes, until al dente. Drain and keep warm.

6. In a large heavy-bottom saucepan, heat the olive oil. Add the chopped garlic and sauté briefly until the garlic sizzles.

7. Add the reserved broccoli rabe and sauté until heated through, about 2 to 3 minutes. Toss in the cooked beans with their liquid and heat for another 2 minutes. Season with salt and pepper to taste.

8. In a large bowl or on a large platter, toss the cooked penne with the bean mixture.

9. Serve with grated cheese.

SERVES 4 TO 6

◆

Fusilli Puttanesca

Quick, hot and spicy ~ the name of this classic pasta sauce translates to "whore's pasta." Not intended to be a characterization of the diner, the name is supposedly a comment on the ease and speed with which this sauce can be made. Another version of the dish's origins refers to the fragrance of the sauce ~ so pungent, its aroma drew clients for the ladies of the night. Fun tales to share with your guests (or not); just be sure to share the sauce.

3 tablespoons extra virgin olive oil
3 anchovy fillets
2 dried chili peppers, minced, or
    1 to 2 teaspoons crushed red pepper flakes
2 tablespoons capers
7 cloves garlic, minced
12 oil-cured black olives

1 can Italian style, whole, plum tomatoes
    (28 ounces)
fresh ground black pepper to taste
2 tablespoons dried oregano
7 fresh basil leaves
1 to 1½ pounds fusilli
1 tablespoon salt

1. Heat olive oil in a large saucepan over high heat. Add the anchovies and let them dissolve in the oil for a minute.

2. Add the chilis, capers, garlic, and olives. Stir and cook for about a minute.

3. Drain the liquid from the tomatoes into the saucepan. Coarsely chop the tomatoes or squeeze with your hand into the saucepan. Stir to heat through, season with black pepper, and lower the heat to medium.

4. Add the oregano to the sauce by rubbing it between your hands and dropping it into the tomato mixture. Tear the basil leaves into the sauce. Stir and taste. Correct seasoning.

5. Bring 6 quarts water to a boil. Add salt. Add the pasta to the boiling water and cook until al dente, drain, and toss with a bit of the sauce to keep it from sticking.

6. Divide the pasta onto four or more plates and dress with the rest of the sauce.

SERVES 4 TO 6

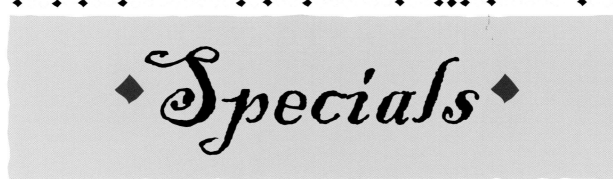

◆ Island Fish Stew ◆

◆ ◆ ◆ ◆ ◆

It's been said that The Black Dog was built because our fearless leader, Capt. Douglas, couldn't find a good cup of fish chowder anywhere. This even heartier fish stew also has the Captain's approval.

5 cloves garlic, minced
3 tablespoons extra virgin olive oil
1 white onion, sliced
2 carrots, julienned
1 leek, well washed and sliced
½ cup dry white wine
1 can (28 ounces) Italian-style crushed tomatoes
1 teaspoon Spanish thread saffron
1 quart fish stock (see page 43)

8 ounces of whitefish (halibut or cod) cut into 1½-inch pieces
1 pound mussels, scrubbed
1 pound littlenecks, scrubbed
½ pound scallops
6 large shrimp, peeled and deveined (see page 96)
¼ pound cleaned squid (see page 69), cut bodies into rings, leave tentacles whole

1. In a large heavy-bottomed pot, heat the olive oil. Add the garlic and sauté slowly.

2. Add the onion, carrots and leek and continue to sauté for about two minutes.

3. Pour in the white wine, stir to blend, and add the tomatoes. Bring to a simmer and add the saffron.

4. Add the fish stock and simmer ten to fifteen minutes.

5. Add the mussels, littlenecks, whitefish, and scallops and bring to a boil.

7. Lower to a simmer, add the shrimp and squid, cover, and let stand for five minutes.

8. Ladle into deep bowls and serve with toasted crusty bread drizzled with olive oil.

SERVES 4

◆

How to Prep Shrimp

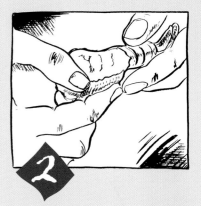

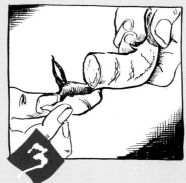

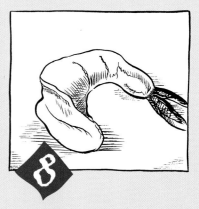

1 The whole shrimp with head removed.

2 Peel back the shell around the body.

3 Remove shell to tail segment.

4 Reserve shell for shrimp stock.

5 Start cutting shrimp from tail to head.

6 Lift up dark vein with your knife.

7 Remove vein.

8 The finished shrimp, ready to use.

◆ Jalapeño Shrimp Quesadillas ◆
WITH ROASTED CORN SALSA

◆ ◆ ◆ ◆ ◆

Prepare this tasty lunch at the end of August when bell peppers, in all their bright colors, are bountiful. You can substitute grilled chicken for the shrimp, if you prefer.

ROASTED CORN SALSA

3 ears of corn
1 red pepper, diced
1 red onion, diced
1 jalapeño, minced

2 tomatoes, diced
½ bunch cilantro, chopped
½ cup red wine vinegar
2 tablespoons canola oil

1. Roast the ears of corn under a hot broiler or on a hot charcoal grill until the kernels are slightly browned. This should take about 5 minutes, but check frequently to make sure the corn isn't burning. After the ears are cool enough to handle, remove the browned kernels by running a knife lengthwise down the cob.

2. In a small bowl, mix together the corn and remaining ingredients. Toss well, cover and chill.

QUESADILLAS

2 red onions
2 red bell peppers
2 yellow bell peppers
1 green bell pepper
4 jalapeño peppers

2 tablespoons canola oil
12 to 16 large shrimp, peeled
    and deveined, see page 96
16 to 20 flour tortillas
2 cups shredded cheddar cheese

1. Prepare the onions and bell peppers by cutting them into strips about 1 inch in length. Carefully remove the seeds from the jalapeños and dice them. (Make sure not to touch your face, and wash your hands immediately after handling these peppers.)

2. To cook the quesadilla filling, heat the canola oil in a large sauté pan. Add the onion and all the peppers and sauté until the peppers are soft. Add the shrimp and cook for about 3 to 5 minutes, until pink.

3. Spread ½ cup or more of the quesadilla filling on a tortilla, cover with shredded cheese and top with another tortilla. Continue assembling quesadillas until you have used all the filling and cheese.

4. Place in a large non-stick skillet and cook until lightly browned, about 2 minutes. Turn over and cover. Continue cooking for about another 4 minutes. If you prefer, you can bake these on a non-stick cookie sheet for about 6 to 8 minutes in a 450°F oven. Baked quesadillas will be less moist than fried ones.

5. Serve, cut in wedges, with Roasted Corn Salsa.

SERVES 4 TO 6

◆ Stir~Fried Spicy Shrimp ◆

◆◆◆◆◆

*Lots of shrimp and veggies make a quick and delicious meal ~ once you've
done the prep. Don't heat that wok until you're ready.*

STIR-FRY INGREDIENTS

24 large shrimp
4 bok choy stalks
3 celery stalks
1 red bell pepper
2 carrots
2 tablespoons vegetable oil
2 teaspoons sesame oil
1 tablespoon chopped fresh ginger
5 cloves garlic, chopped
5 scallions, chopped

SPICY SAUCE MIX

2 tablespoons chili paste
  with garlic
¼ cup dry sherry
2 tablespoons hoisin sauce
1 tablespoon sugar

RICE

your choice of cooked rice:
  white or brown

1. Peel and devein the shrimp (see "How To Prep Shrimp" on page 96).

2. Prepare the veggies. Chop the bok choy stalks, leaves and stems into 2-inch pieces and cut the celery stalks into ¼-inch sections. Chop the red pepper into 1-inch strips, slice the carrots lengthwise and cut in 2-inch sections.

3. Place a wok or deep heavy sauté pan over high heat. Add the vegetable and sesame oil.

4. Add the ginger, garlic and scallions and stir-fry quickly.

5. Add the shrimp and stir-fry for about 3 minutes to cook through.

6. Now add the red pepper, celery and bok choy one at a time, tossing each addition to coat with the hot oil.

7. Cover and cook for about 2 minutes.

8. While the shrimp and vegetables are cooking, combine the spicy sauce mixture in a small bowl.

9. Now pour the spicy sauce into the wok and cook briefly to heat through.

10. Serve with rice on the side.

SERVES 4

◆ Grilled Marinated Shrimp ◆

◆ ◆ ◆ ◆ ◆

Summer, the season to cook outdoors. Choose this recipe for easy entertaining. Great served with a pitcher of margaritas.

⅓ cup extra virgin olive oil
¼ cup fresh lime juice
2 cloves garlic, crushed
2 tablespoons chopped fresh cilantro
2 tablespoons Worcestershire sauce

1 teaspoon Tabasco sauce
salt and pepper to taste
24 large shrimp, shell on
lime wedges for garnish

1. Mix together the olive oil, lime juice, and seasonings in a medium size bowl.

2. Split the shrimp up the back with a sharp knife to allow the marinade to penetrate. Leave the shell on, but remove the vein if it looks gross.

3. Add the raw shrimp to the marinade and refrigerate, covered, for about two to three hours.

4. Remove from the marinade and grill over hot coals for four to five minutes, until done. The shrimp may also be broiled. This takes about eight minutes.

5. Serve on a platter with lime wedges. Peel and eat!

SERVES 4

◆ Steamed Mussels ◆

◆ ◆ ◆ ◆ ◆

A favorite lunch at The Black Dog. We serve a large platter per person with garlic bread and a bountiful salad. When buying mussels, figure on at least 1 pound per person and make sure all the mussels' shells are intact and tightly closed.

2 pounds well-scrubbed mussels
2 tablespoons olive oil
2 tablespoons chopped garlic
2 tablespoons chopped onion
1 tablespoon chopped parsley
1 cup chopped tomatoes
1½ cups dry white wine
juice of ½ lemon
1 teaspoon salt
½ teaspoon pepper
Garlic bread

1. Scrub your mussels under running water, removing any beards. Discard any mussels with shells that are broken or not tightly closed.

2. In a large pot, heat the olive oil. Add the garlic and onion and sauté briefly, for about 2 minutes.

3. Now add the mussels, tomatoes, parsley, wine, lemon juice, salt and pepper. Stir to combine ingredients.

4. Cover the pot and increase the temperature to high. The mussels should steam open in about 5 minutes.

5. Serve with the cooking liquor and slices of warm garlic bread.

SERVES 2

◆   ◆   ◆

◆ Squid Happens ◆

A sign that spring is actually here is the arrival of squid in the harbors. Although jigging squid is a favorite Island pastime, most people don't know quite what to do with the creatures. The rule of thumb is cook squid either in a flash (about a minute) or for a long time (past the rubbery stage). Here's an easy recipe.

1 small onion
1 green pepper
1 small bulb fresh fennel
1 cup baby artichokes
1/4 cup extra virgin olive oil
4 to 6 cloves garlic, diced
1 cup white wine
1 28-ounce can crushed tomatoes
1 teaspoon oregano
1 teaspoon basil
1 teaspoon thyme
1/4 teaspoon crushed red pepper
1 pound cleaned squid, cut into rings
  (See "How to Clean Squid"
  on page 69)
salt and pepper
1 pound pasta

1. Thinly slice all the vegetables.

2. Heat the olive oil in a saucepan and add the vegetables and garlic. Sauté until tender.

3. Add the wine, tomatoes, herbs, crushed red pepper, and squid. Bring to a simmer.

4. Cover and simmer for about 45 minutes, stirring occasionally.

5. Adjust seasoning.

6. Serve over your favorite pasta.

SERVES 4 TO 6

◆ Littlenecks with ◆ Spicy Black Bean Sauce

◆ ◆ ◆ ◆ ◆

Whether you want a spicy appetizer or hearty lunch, this easy stir-fry assembles in minutes. The key ingredient, black beans in a salty paste, used to be a little difficult to find but now most large grocery stores stock jars of it in their specialty food sections.

2 tablespoons salted black beans
2 tablespoons vegetable oil
1 teaspoon dark sesame oil
4 cloves of garlic, minced
2 chopped fresh small Thai chilis or
  1 teaspoon red pepper flakes
3 scallions, chopped

¼ pound ground pork
¼ to ½ teaspoon white pepper
24 littlenecks, scrubbed
¼ cup dry sherry
1 cup chicken stock (see page 44)
1 tablespoon tamari
your favorite cooked rice

1. Soak the salted black beans in hot water to soften for about 10 minutes. Then drain and rinse under running water and reserve.

2. Heat a wok or large heavy saucepan over high heat and add the vegetable and sesame oils.

3. Add the garlic, chilis and scallions and stir-fry for about a minute, being careful not to burn the garlic.

4. Add the ground pork and stir-fry until the pork is browned, about 3 minutes.

5. Add the salted black beans and white pepper to your taste.

6. Now put the scrubbed littlenecks into the wok and stir fry to coat with the pork and black bean mixture.

7. Add the sherry and stir a minute and then add the chicken stock and tamari.

8. Cover the wok or saucepan and cook over high heat until the littlenecks steam open. This should take about 5 to 7 minutes.

9. Serve over rice.

SERVES 4 AS AN APPETIZER OR 2 FOR LUNCH

◆

◆ Grilled Beef Fajitas ◆

◆ ◆ ◆ ◆ ◆

Eating fajitas is a fun summer group activity. They're perfect for an outdoor barbecue or indoor casual gathering where guests can assemble their own meal. For the Southwestern Rub, you can substitute a pre-made Cajun spice blend with good results. The beef will have more intense flavor if you allow it to marinate in the dry rub for several hours under refrigeration. The salsa can be made ahead of time, or you can use your favorite salsa recipe.

FRESH SALSA

4 ripe tomatoes
1 red onion
1 jalapeño pepper
2 tablespoons lemon juice

1 small bunch of
  fresh cilantro or fresh mint
salt and pepper to taste

1. Core the tomatoes and peel the onion.

2. Rough chop the tomatoes, onion, and jalapeño. Use caution with the jalapeño and keep your hands away from your eyes.

3. Place in food processor with lemon juice and blend briefly for a coarse salsa.

4. Add chopped cilantro or mint if desired.

5. Add salt and pepper to taste. Set aside to let the flavors blend.

SOUTHWESTERN SPICE RUB

2 tablespoons paprika
2 teaspoons cumin
2 teaspoons cayenne
2 tablespoons chili powder

2 teaspoons onion powder
2 teaspoons garlic powder
1 tablespoon powdered thyme
1 tablespoon powdered marjoram

FAJITAS

2 pounds flank steak, skirt steak,
  or sirloin tips
2 medium onions
2 to 3 mixed peppers

2 tablespoons olive oil
1 dozen large flour tortillas
1 cup sour cream

1. Mix spice rub ingredients, cover the beef with the rub, and set aside.

2. Peel and slice the onions. Remove the seeds from the peppers and slice. Cook the onions and peppers in olive oil in a cast iron pan until they are slightly wilted.

3. Grill the beef over coals if barbecuing, or in a cast iron pan if indoors, to your desired doneness. We prefer about seven minutes for medium rare.

4. Warm up tortillas by heating on a dry pan or grill.

5. Slice the beef across the grain in about half-inch slices.

6. Serve with warm tortillas, the pepper and onion salsa, and sour cream on the side.

SERVES 4 TO 6

Spicy Stir~Fried Vegetables with Tofu & Peanuts

At The Black Dog, stir-fry dishes are so popular that Charlie, who created this dish, actually suffered from "wok" elbow for a time. Take the time to prep everything and then the meal assembles in a flash.

STIR-FRY SAUCE

1 tablespoon chili paste with garlic
1 tablespoon hot bean sauce
2 tablespoons rice wine vinegar
2 tablespoons dry white sherry
1 tablespoon sugar

STIR-FRY INGREDIENTS

$\frac{1}{2}$ cup broccoli florets
4 celery stalks
4 bok choy stalks
1 red bell pepper
3 Thai chilis or other fresh hot peppers
1 pound firm tofu
1 cup peanut oil
3 tablespoons vegetable oil
1 teaspoon sesame oil
$\frac{1}{2}$ cup raw shelled peanuts
3 cloves of garlic, minced
4 scallions, chopped
white pepper
2 cups mung bean sprouts
Your choice of cooked rice or noodles

1. Blend together the sauce ingredients in a small bowl and reserve.

2. Chop the celery and pepper in $\frac{1}{2}$-inch pieces. Cut the stems of the bok choy in julienne strips and shred the leaves. Seed and chop the chilis. (Keep your hands away from your face; peppers burn!)

3. Cut the tofu into small triangles. Heat the peanut oil in a wok and deep-fry the tofu until golden but not dry. Drain and reserve the tofu. Discard the oil.

4. Heat your wok and add the vegetable and sesame oils. Add the raw peanuts and stir-fry for about 1 to 2 minutes. Add the garlic, chilis, scallions, and white pepper. Quickly add the broccoli, celery, bok choy, red pepper, sprouts and tofu triangles. Stir-fry for 4 to 5 minutes. Pour the sauce over the wok mixture and stir-fry to blend.

5. Serve over rice or noodles.

SERVES 4 TO 6

ANOTHER SUMMER SEASON is over and the last softball game has been played. The Brew Crew is just a memory and Dumpy was scrapped long ago. Leo still travels off-Island but Zipperhead has remained in his homeland. When you stop by for breakfast, Happy Heff and Uncle Al are still on the line and Oh and the Oh'ettes have returned for an encore. Zippy, the Tin Man, is practicing law and Two Scram Pam has left the scene. We're all grateful that Norman Bates left the dishroom. Derby time is approaching so Fish will be out casting. The Queens have disbanded but the Dough Boy is still calling meetings. We think fondly of the Brown Rice Lady and now use the volume control on the stereo since McSterminator and his cleaver have left the building. Need a translation? Ask Jack (a/k/a Fish), the instigator of this madness, or Rick, who has been known as Leo for so long, that's even what his mother calls him. When you join The Black Dog crew, you are given a "nom de chien" whether you like it or not. I'm still trying to change mine from Grumpy.

~E.S.

◆ "Buffa~Leo" Wings ◆

◆ ◆ ◆ ◆

If you look at the ingredients in Leo's recipe, you'd think that these wings would be seriously hot ~ not true. Of course, if heat is what you want, choose your hot sauce accordingly. Leo uses a lot of butter in this sauce, because that's what allows the sauce to adhere to the wings and carries the flavor. You can reduce the butter if you like.

48 chicken wings
2 sticks butter (1/2 pound)
2 cups of your favorite hot sauce
1 ounce Tabasco Sauce
1 tablespoon cayenne pepper
1 tablespoon white pepper
1 teaspoon black pepper

1/2 cup carrot juice
1 tablespoon minced garlic
1 jalapeño pepper
vegetable oil for deep frying
blue cheese dressing (your favorite recipe)
4 celery stalks, julienned

1. Cut chicken wings at the joints into three sections reserving the tips for chicken stock. Set aside.

2. To prepare the sauce, melt butter and stir in the hot sauce, the Tabasco, the cayenne, white and black peppers, the carrot juice, and the garlic. Float the whole jalapeño in the sauce. Set aside.

3. Heat two inches of oil in a cast iron pan, wok, or heavy saucepan. If you own an electric fryer use per instructions. Heat oil to 375°F. If you don't have a thermometer, test the oil by dipping part of a chicken wing into it. It should sizzle if ready.

4. Deep fry wings, a small batch at a time, until done, about five minutes. To test for doneness, cut open a wing and make sure that there's no pink inside. Drain on paper towels.

5. Toss the fried wings in the sauce to coat and serve with the blue cheese dressing and celery sticks.

SERVES 6 TO 8

You are where you eat.
~ ANONYMOUS

Dinner

Starters

Pasta

Entrées

Vegetables

COMING BACK to the Island at night, winter or summer, you can spot the Tavern on the beach from the ferry deck as you enter Vineyard Haven harbor. With candles alight in the windows, it offers a warm welcome home. Inside, there's a pause in conversation as the light of the ferry beacon illuminates the beach and harbor, and all are once again reminded of the beauty around them. We are lucky to be in such a magical place, and our cooks (also known as the "dinner gods") offer fare to match. Dinner at The Black Dog defines comfort in every respect ~ from your own (wear what you like) ~ to your choice of wine (bring it to drink it). You may not be able to duplicate our location, but our recipes will bring a bit of the flavor of The Black Dog to the comfort of your home.

Starters

◆ Baba Ganouj ◆

Whether you spell it with "j" or "sh" or some other way, there are just as many versions of the ingredients necessary to make a great Baba Ganouj as there are spellings of this classic Middle Eastern starter. We like it with yogurt and lots of garlic.

1 large eggplant
4 cloves garlic
1 teaspoon plus 2 tablespoons olive oil
1 teaspoon salt
½ cup plain yogurt
⅓ cup tahini

juice of 1 to 2 lemons
½ teaspoon fresh ground black pepper
½ teaspoon ground cumin

pita points
sprouts

1. Preheat the oven to 400°F. Prepare a baking tray, jelly roll pan, or shallow roasting pan by oiling it with about ½ teaspoon olive oil.

2. Place the eggplant on the baking tray and prick with a fork numerous times to create vent holes for steam. Drizzle ½ teaspoon of olive oil on the garlic cloves and add to tray.

3. Put the baking tray into the oven, and roast for about 8 minutes, then remove the garlic and set aside to cool. Continue roasting the eggplant for an additional 45 minutes or so until the eggplant has "deflated."

4. Remove from the oven and let it cool. Once the eggplant is cool enough to handle, scoop the pulp out into a bowl.

5. Peel and mash the roasted garlic cloves with the salt and add to the eggplant. Mix in the remaining ingredients, including 2 tablespoons of olive oil, adding enough lemon juice to maintain a smooth consistency.

6. Chill covered for about 30 minutes.

7. Serve with toasted pita bread triangles and sprouts.

SERVES 6 TO 8

◆

◆ Hummus ◆

◆ ◆ ◆ ◆ ◆

Black Dog cooks love tahini, so it makes sense that hummus would also appear on our menu. We make our version of this classic Middle Eastern dip with lots of garlic (surprised?) and a dash of cayenne, although you may substitute cumin if you prefer. Just take some chickpeas, or garbanzos as the California kids call them, and mix it all up. Easy and very tasty.

2 cups cooked chickpeas (either
   canned or cook ½ pound dry
   to yield 2 cups)
3 garlic cloves, minced
½ cup tahini
juice of 1 lemon
½ cup olive oil
1 teaspoon salt
½ teaspoon black pepper
dash of cayenne

toasted pita points

1. To prepare dried chickpeas, clean and soak ½ pound
   overnight. The next day, rinse them and put in a large pot covered with water. Bring to
   a boil, add about 1 teaspoon of salt and cook at a simmer for around 2 hours, until they are
   soft. Drain, reserving a little of the cooking liquid. The easy way is to buy cooked canned
   chickpeas, drain, reserve the can liquid, and rinse.

2. Place cooked chickpeas in a food processor and pulse briefly.

3. Add the garlic, tahini (remember to mix it up first, since it often separates), lemon juice,
   olive oil, and seasonings. Continue to process until the mixture achieves a smooth
   consistency. If it's too thick, add a little of the reserved cooking liquid or can liquid. Place
   in a bowl and chill.

4. To serve, drizzle with a little olive oil and surround it with your favorite raw veggies and
   toasted pita points.

SERVES 8 TO 10   ◆

Sweet Corn Pepper Salsa

◆ ◆ ◆ ◆ ◆

Just-picked corn truly is sweet, but it doesn't take long for the sugars to turn to starch. If only older ears are available, we recommend "roasting" them first for added flavor. This salsa is great with grilled fish and chicken or just grab the chips.

4 ears freshly picked corn
1 red pepper, diced
1 green jalapeño pepper, minced
1 small bunch of cilantro, chopped
1 small red onion, chopped
½ cup fresh lime juice
¼ cup sherry vinegar
¼ cup olive oil
3 cloves of garlic, minced
salt and pepper to taste

1. Cut the kernels from the fresh corn ears. (Grill older ears for 3 to 5 minutes, or put them under the broiler for 10 to 15 minutes.)
2. Mix all the ingredients together in a medium-size bowl. Cover and refrigerate for at least an hour to let the flavors develop.

YIELDS: 3 CUPS

◆ Steamers ◆
THE FUNDAMENTALS

◆◆◆◆◆

Steamers, or steamed clams, are also known as soft-shell clams. That's because their shells can be cracked easily, unlike their hard-shell relatives known as quahogs. Steamers have elongated bodies and a protruding neck with a skin you should remove before eating. Digging them, "clamming," can be a test of will ~ yours. You can't believe how fast a clam can bury itself to elude its fate. If you know how to dig for clams, you surely know how to prepare them. These ten steps are for those of you who just bought some or had them gifted (lucky you!).

1. Figure on one pound of clams per person.

2. Soak clams (unopened) for a few hours in a bucket of salted water ~ enough to completely cover them. This should purge them of sand. You can add 1 tablespoon of cornmeal to the water. That often helps the clams give up their sand.

3. Discard any clams that float to the surface.

4. Bring one inch of water to a boil in a pot large enough to hold all of your clams. Season the water with a squeeze of fresh lemon juice, about 1 tablespoon.

5. Place the clams in this pot and cover.

6. Melt butter.

7. Keep the clams on the heat until the pot froths, and clams open, then **IMMEDIATELY** remove the pot from the burner. This should take about 5 minutes for a pound of clams, longer for larger quantities.

8. Drain the clams, reserving the cooking liquid. This is your broth.

9. For each serving offer a bowl of steamers, a mug of the reserved broth, and a container of melted butter.

10. To eat, remove the clam from its shell (this should be easy), discard the skin around the neck. Dunk the rest first in the broth and then the melted butter. Enjoy!

Note: Some drink the broth after finishing the clams. It's salty but tasty ~ just don't drain your mug to the last drop or you'll be chewing a bit of sand.

◆

How to Open a Clam

1 Place the clam in your left hand with the hinge facing down and the lips facing your fingers.

2 Press the knife into the clam using pressure from the fingers of your left hand.

3 Once inside, cut one-third of the way into the clam.

4 Twist the knife. That should cut and separate the first muscle.

5 Retract the knife and run the knife along the inside of the top shell.

6 Pull back the top shell. Cut under the clam in the bottom shell to remove the clam.

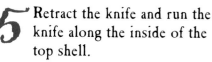

◆ Black Dog Stuffed Quahogs ◆

◆ ◆ ◆ ◆ ◆

This traditional and substantial appetizer served in its own shell makes a tasty start to any meal ~ especially one featuring seafood. You can vary the flavor by using sausage (we use Andouille) instead of bacon. For extra zing, add a diced jalapeño to the veggie sauté.

8 slices bread
8 slices of bacon, chopped into ½-inch pieces
½ teaspoon crushed red pepper flakes
2 chopped garlic cloves
1 medium white onion, diced
1 medium green bell pepper, diced
6 large quahogs, opened and chopped with juice and shells
   (see "How to Open a Clam," page 118)
1 tablespoon fresh parsley, chopped
1 teaspoon ground black pepper
garnish: lime and lemon wedges

1. Dice the bread slices into ½-inch cubes and dry overnight or in an oven at 300°F for about 10 minutes.

2. In a large heavy-bottomed skillet, cook the chopped bacon. When the bacon is just browned, add the crushed red pepper and garlic. Sauté for 1 minute.

3. Add the diced veggies and continue to sauté for 3 to 4 minutes until the onion and pepper are just soft.

4. Add the chopped clam meat and reserved clam juice and cook for 3 to 4 minutes. The mixture should boil.

5. Remove from heat and stir in the dried bread cubes, parsley, and black pepper. Allow the mixture to cool a bit before stuffing into shells. Preheat the oven to 400°F.

6. Make sure the clamshells are clean. Mound the mixture into each half shell and place the filled shells on a baking tray.

7. Baked stuffed quahogs for 20 to 25 minutes or until nicely browned on top.

8. Serve with lemon and lime wedges.

YIELDS: 12

◆

Grill It

Grilling food at **The Black Dog** is a year 'round activity, but when it comes to cooking at home ~ most of us only use a grill outdoors during mild weather. This section offers some ideas and some great marinades to add flavor and tenderness to your next grilling adventure. You can find many other recipes for dishes to cook on a grill throughout the lunch and dinner sections of this cookbook.

Do's

- Set up your grill downwind from the party, if possible.
- Think through your set-up ~ can guests circulate around serving tables?
- Gather appropriate utensils and plenty of towels before starting.
- Make sure you have a spray bottle filled with water to control flare-ups.
- Use a clean, hot grill.
- Season everything with salt and pepper, at least, but experiment with herb blends, rubs, jerks and marinades.
- Rub a small amount of oil on items before grilling to prevent sticking.
- Wrap more delicate items in foil or use a grill basket to hold them.
- Soak all wooden skewers in water before using.
- Skewer smaller items for easier handling ~ mushrooms, scallops, shrimp.
- Soak cornhusks in water before grilling ears (don't forget to remove corn silk).
- Consider partially cooking whole poultry and bone-in pork to reduce grilling time.
- Have fun, play music, enjoy some of your favorite beverage.
- Some of the best dishes happen by accident.
- Recruit some help.
- Assume nothing.

Don'ts

- Use the same platter for raw and cooked items.
- Overcook ~ you can always cook it more, never less.
- Pour lighter fluid on wood or charcoal while food is grilling.
- Cook on flames ~ always wait to cook until you have glowing coals.
- Use aerosol oils on a hot grill.
- Create dead-end paths in your serving area.

◆ Easy Grill Marinade ◆
FOR POULTRY, FISH, VEGETABLES OR MEAT

◆ ◆ ◆ ◆ ◆

Because this all-purpose marinade is highly acidic, it gives an almost "cooked" appearance to the exterior of just about any meat, poultry or fish if you leave the item in it for an extended period of time. Don't be fooled by appearance and alter cooking times. If you want to use this marinade on white fish, omit the red wine vinegar.

1 cup olive oil
½ cup fresh lemon juice
¼ cup red wine vinegar
1 tablespoon parsley, chopped
¼ cup fresh basil, chopped

¼ cup fresh rosemary, chopped
8 garlic cloves, minced
1 tablespoon salt
2 teaspoons fresh ground black pepper

Mix together all the ingredients and marinate your grilling choice in a large glass container, covered, under refrigeration.

YIELDS: 2 CUPS

VARIATIONS ~

• Use a different vinegar: balsamic, sherry or rice wine.

• Use different herbs: chervil, tarragon, cilantro.

• Sweeten it: add brown sugar or honey.

• Spice it: add crushed red pepper flakes, chipotle powder, minced jalapeño or other fresh hot pepper.

RULES OF THUMB ~

• Marinate tougher meats or large cuts for 1 to 2 days.

• Marinate smaller or more tender cuts of meat or poultry from 1 to 8 hours.

• Marinate large cuts of fish up to 1 hour.

• Brush marinade on smaller pieces of fish while grilling.

• Larger pieces of vegetables can benefit from longer marinating time.

◆

◆ Tamari Lemon Marinade ◆
FOR FISH

◆ ◆ ◆ ◆ ◆

Here's a very simple marinade that can be used on just about anything. Great for grilled fish or meat, it can also be used to season cooked fish or vegetables.

juice of one lemon
1 cup tamari
1 small bunch of scallions
2 eight-ounce portions salmon, bluefish, swordfish, or tuna

1. Chop the scallions and combine with the lemon juice and tamari.

2. Marinate the fish in this mixture for about half an hour.

3. Preheat the grill and oil it to prevent fish from sticking.

4. Grill, basting with the marinade a few times. When using fillets, you should start with the skin side up. A good way to time the fish is to cook ten minutes per inch of thickness. If the fish is one inch thick, then cook it five minutes per side. (When cooking salmon at The Black Dog we prefer to grill it slightly underdone, since it continues to cook briefly after leaving the grill surface.)

SERVES 2

◆

◆ Red Wine Marinade ◆
FOR BEEF

◆ ◆ ◆ ◆ ◆

This mixture will easily marinate a generous amount of steaks ~ it makes about two and half cups of marinade. It's best to leave your meat in the marinade for four to six hours. That will effectively tenderize your beef and add additional flavor. Remember, never cook with wine you would not drink.

2 cloves garlic
2 teaspoons salt
1¼ cups hearty red wine
¾ cups olive oil
¼ cup minced parsley
1 tablespoon minced fresh thyme
1 tablespoon minced savory
2 tablespoons minced chives
2 tablespoons freshly ground pepper

1. Mince the garlic together with the salt until you have a paste-like consistency.

2. Pour the wine into a medium size bowl. Add the garlic/salt mince.

3. Whisk the oil into the wine mixture. Stir in the remaining seasonings and mix thoroughly.

4. Now you're ready to marinate your choice of beef.

YIELDS: 2½ CUPS

◆

Entrées

Greek Marinated Bluefish

⬥⬥⬥⬥⬥

Bluefish are celebrated on the Vineyard both as great eating and great sport. The highlight of the year for our cooks is the Martha's Vineyard Striped Bass and Bluefish Derby, more than fifty years old. One year Oh, chef extraordinaire, caught a 15-pound 14-ounce bluefish at his secret spot just near The Black Dog and won first place. Most of Oh's catch makes it to our menu, but not that one ~ it's on his wall.

2½ pounds of bluefish fillets,
    boned and skinned
½ cup olive oil
juice of one lemon
3 garlic cloves, chopped
salt & pepper
3 tablespoons chopped fresh rosemary
3 tablespoons chopped fresh oregano

5 vine-ripe tomatoes, sliced

1. Preheat oven to 425°F. Rinse the fillets and pat dry. Divide into six equal portions.

2. Place fillets in a shallow dish. Combine olive oil, lemon juice, garlic, salt and pepper. Add half the fresh herbs and pour over fish, making sure each piece is well coated.

3. Marinate under refrigeration for at least one hour.

4. When ready to cook, drain the marinade and bake uncovered for eight to ten minutes, until done. If you prefer, broil the fish instead of baking it.

5. To serve, place the fillets on a bed of sliced tomatoes, sprinkle with remaining fresh herbs, and drizzle with olive oil.

SERVES 6

How to Fillet a Fish

1 With the belly side away from you, cut behind the head to the backbone.

2 Run knife down the back of the fish above the fin bone.

3 Cut towards the tail along the backbone.

4 Peel back the meat while running the knife along the bones.

5 Lift the fillet away from the fish frame.

6 Finished fish fillet.

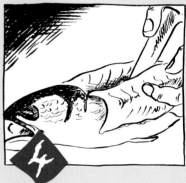

◆ Bluefish Genovese ◆

◆ ◆ ◆ ◆ ◆

Celebrating Genoa, a seaport in a region of Italy long known for the best basil, here's a recipe for our local favorite ~ bluefish. If fresh bluefish is unknown in your area, substitute salmon.

1 pound red new potatoes
7 cloves of garlic
½ cup extra virgin olive oil
1 cup fresh basil leaves
1 teaspoon salt
pepper to taste
2 pounds fresh bluefish fillets
   (skin removed)
juice of 1 lemon
¼ cup water
¼ cup white wine

1. Preheat oven to 425°F.

2. Cut new potatoes into ¼-inch slices. Peel and chop the garlic cloves.

3. Mix the potatoes and chopped garlic together in a roasting pan large enough to hold the bluefish fillets.

4. Toss with half of the olive oil.

5. Tear the basil leaves into thin strips and add to the potato-garlic mixture. Toss with the salt and pepper to taste.

6. Put the roasting pan into the oven for about 20 minutes, baking the potatoes until they are just golden.

7. Remove from the oven and lift out the potatoes and set aside briefly.

8. Place the bluefish fillets in the roasting pan and drizzle with lemon juice. Pour the remaining olive oil over the fillets. Add the water and wine to the pan, surrounding the fish. Cover the fish with the potato mixture.

9. Return the filled roasting pan to the oven and bake for about another 10 minutes, until the potatoes are cooked and the fish can be separated easily with a fork, but is still moist.

10. To serve, divide the fish among plates and serve with the potatoes on the side.

SERVES 4 TO 6

◆

✦ Sesame Crusted Salmon Fillet ✦

✦ ✦ ✦ ✦ ✦

One of the most popular entrées at **The Black Dog**, this quick sauté marries the flavors of salmon and sesame ~ beautifully.

3/4 cup plain bread crumbs
1/2 cup raw white hulled sesame seeds
1/2 teaspoon white pepper
1 teaspoon salt
2 teaspoons Spanish paprika
2 teaspoons chopped fresh parsley
1/4 cup plus 3 teaspoons dark (toasted) sesame oil
2 tablespoons canola oil
2 pounds boneless, skinless salmon fillets, approximately 1 inch thick

1. Mix together the bread crumbs, sesame seeds, white pepper, salt, paprika, parsley, and 1/4 cup of the sesame oil.

2. Place a sauté pan over medium high heat and add the canola oil.

3. Rub about 1 teaspoon of sesame oil on the top of each fillet, making sure it is well covered. Press fillets into the bread crumb mixture to coat well.

4. Place the breaded salmon, crumb side down, in the hot pan and sear for about 5 minutes or until evenly browned.

5. Turn the fillet over and finish cooking on the other side for about 5 minutes more.

6. Serve over Chilled Sesame Spinach, see page 186.

SERVES 4 TO 6

✦

Pan~Seared Codfish with Creamy Lobster Sauce

◆ ◆ ◆ ◆ ◆

At night, The Black Dog mellows into a scene of candlelight reflecting on burnished copper and warm wood. Folks sitting on the porch catch first sight of ferries approaching the Island by their bright beacons. Could be called romantic ~ just like this beautiful and delicious feast. You have candles, why not make your own mellow evening?

CREAMY LOBSTER SAUCE

1 chicken lobster (1-pound lobster)
1 small carrot, diced
1 small white onion, diced
2 sprigs fresh thyme
2 teaspoons canola oil

¼ cup dry sherry
⅔ cup heavy cream
1 teaspoon tomato paste
salt and white pepper to taste

1. Steam the lobster (see "Lobster: The Fundamentals," page 149). Cool, and remove the meat, reserving the shells. Chop the shells into small pieces. Chop the lobster tail meat into bite-size portions. Reserve the large claw meat for garnish. Don't forget to include the sweet meat from the knuckles. Chill the lobster meat.

2. In a large, heavy-bottomed saucepan sauté the diced vegetables and thyme in oil until the onions begin to brown. Add the broken lobster shells and body.

3. Pour in the sherry to deglaze the pan. Simmer to reduce the volume by half.

4. Add the heavy cream and bring to a boil. Reduce the heat to medium and continue cooking until the volume is reduced by one third.

5. Add the tomato paste and mix well. Add salt and white pepper to taste.

6. Strain this sauce into a small bowl through a fine sieve, using a spoon to press the mixture against the side to yield the most sauce.

7. Add the chopped lobster meat to the sauce and adjust seasoning.

YIELDS: APPROXIMATELY 1 CUP WITH LOBSTER MEAT

THE FISH

1 tablespoon canola oil
2 teaspoons fresh parsley, chopped
½ teaspoon salt
¼ teaspoon ground black pepper
2 teaspoons extra virgin olive oil

2 boneless, skinless codfish fillets
(about 8 ounces each, 1-inch to
1½-inch thick)

1. Preheat a heavy-bottomed skillet on high. Add canola oil and heat.

2. Mix together the parsley, salt and pepper. Drizzle the olive oil on top of the fish and sprinkle liberally with parsley mixture.

3. Place the seasoned fish parsley-side down into the hot pan. Reduce the heat to medium high and allow the fish to set. Turn the pan to make sure that you are achieving even cooking. Do not turn the fish for three to four minutes. Once a nice sear has been achieved turn over the fillets and sear the opposite side for four minutes more.

4. Heat two plates and place a fillet partially covered with lobster sauce on each. Garnish with reserved claw meat.

SERVES 2

◆

◆ Garlic Crusted Codfish ◆

◆ ◆ ◆ ◆ ◆

It's hard to believe that something so delicious takes so little time. Just bring home the codfish ~ you probably have everything else on hand.

1 tablespoon butter
2 tablespoons olive oil
6 cloves garlic, chopped
1 cup bread crumbs
1/4 cup chopped parsley
1/4 teaspoon salt
1/4 teaspoon ground black pepper
1 egg, beaten
2 pounds boneless 1-inch-thick codfish fillets, cut into four pieces
4 lemon wedges

1. Preheat oven to 400°F. Heat butter and oil in a saucepan on low heat and add the garlic for one minute to soften, not brown.

2. Remove pan from heat and add the bread crumbs, parsley, salt and pepper. Mix to moisten crumbs and seasoning.

3. Dredge each fillet in the beaten egg first, then the crumb mixture, and place in an oiled roasting pan.

4. Bake fillets in the preheated oven for about ten to twelve minutes. The crust should be golden brown. The fish inside will be moist and flaky.

5. Serve with lemon wedges.

SERVES 4

Overheard

AT THE BLACK DOG:

PATRON:
"What's your house wine?"

STAFF:
"It's a dry town."

PATRON:
"That sounds good....
I'll have a glass."

Bubba's Bonito

◆ ◆ ◆ ◆ ◆

If you work at The Black Dog, you don't make any vacation plans in August. That's the month when the Island swells with visitors and our student help departs for classes. A few years back, Jack had to take his own daughter off to college, so he left in August. That year President Clinton and his family came to The Black Dog for dinner for the first time. When Jack returned to find he had missed all the hoopla, his response was, "The President can come in anytime, but you can only take your daughter to college for the first time once." In any case, he came back ~ the President, that is ~ and Jack renamed this dish.

1 large red onion, sliced
1 red bell pepper, sliced
1 green bell pepper, sliced
1 yellow bell pepper, sliced
3 to 4 cloves of garlic, minced
1 cup extra virgin olive oil
1 sprig fresh rosemary
½ cup balsamic vinegar
1 tablespoon vegetable oil
2 pounds bonito fillets (or tuna steaks)

TO PREPARE PEPPER COMBO

1. In a medium saucepan, sauté the sliced onion, peppers, and minced garlic in 2 tablespoons of the olive oil for about 5 minutes.

2. Remove from heat and place in a bowl.

3. Chop the rosemary and add it to the bowl along with the balsamic vinegar and remaining olive oil.

4. Toss lightly and chill for about an hour.

TO PREPARE BONITO

1. Preheat grill and brush it with the vegetable oil.
2. Cut fillets in 4 pieces and place flesh side down for about 3 minutes. Flip and cook for about 2 more minutes.
3. Serve each fillet covered with the chilled pepper combo.

SERVES 4 TO 6

"Fish"

OUR EXECUTIVE CHEF, Jack, is also known as "Fish," because when he's not at the Tavern cutting or preparing fish, he's out fishing! That's why the fish on our menu is only hours from the sea. He's kept it that way for more than twenty years, as the scrapbook photos attest. Gotta love it!

Baked Striped Bass with Braised Fennel

◆ ◆ ◆ ◆ ◆

A prized game fish, the striped bass has always been a favorite of Black Dog patrons. Along the Atlantic coast it was almost loved to extinction. For nearly ten years, Black Dog cooks retired their striped bass recipes, doing their bit early-on to stop the decline of this delicious fish. We're all lucky to report that because of the timely action of the state and with the cooperation of sport and commercial fishermen, the once-overfished striped bass is now abundant, a model of what can be done.

1 fennel bulb, thinly sliced
3 tablespoons butter
1 cup stock (fish or chicken,
   see pages 43 and 44)

2 pounds striped bass fillets
1 cup white wine
1/4 cup fresh lemon juice
salt and pepper

1. Preheat oven to 375°F. In a medium saucepan, sauté fennel in butter for about 5 minutes.

2. Pour in stock and continue simmering until the fennel is tender and the liquid has reduced by half. This should take about 15 to 20 minutes.

3. While the fennel is cooking, place fish in a shallow baking pan with white wine and lemon juice.

4. Bake the striped bass for about ten minutes per inch of thickness.

5. When the fennel is tender, add salt and pepper to taste.

6. Serve fish fillet on a platter with fennel and sauce.

SERVES 4 TO 6

Sautéed Striped Bass with Garlic Mustard Sauce

◆ ◆ ◆ ◆ ◆

This is a tasty, simple way to prepare any firm-fleshed fish. If striped bass isn't available you can substitute sea bass, halibut, or red snapper to name a few.

THE FISH

2 pounds striped bass fillets, skinned and boned
¼ cup flour
1 teaspoon salt
1 teaspoon pepper
2 eggs, lightly beaten
1 tablespoon unsalted butter
¼ cup olive oil

THE SAUCE

7 tablespoons unsalted butter
4 cloves of garlic, crushed
¼ cup Dijon mustard
2 teaspoons lemon zest

1. Preheat oven to 375°F. Cut fish fillets into four equal eight-ounce portions.

2. Combine flour, salt and pepper in one dish and the beaten eggs in another.

3. Melt 1 tablespoon of butter in a saucepan and add the olive oil. Heat until hot.

4. Dredge the fish in flour mixture, shake off the excess, and then dip in the beaten egg.

5. Add the fish fillets to the pan one at a time and sauté until golden brown on both sides. Remove from pan and assemble fillets in a baking dish.

6. Bake for about 8 to 10 minutes.

7. While the fillets are baking, prepare the garlic mustard sauce. Wipe out the olive oil and melt 7 tablespoons butter in the saucepan.

8. Add the crushed garlic, mustard, and lemon zest. Whisk in the pan until blended and continue stirring for about two minutes over medium heat.

9. Serve each fillet with a generous dollop of sauce.

SERVES 4 TO 6

◆

◆ Pan~Seared Red Snapper ◆
WITH WILTED GREENS & GRILLED ROMA TOMATOES

◆ ◆ ◆ ◆ ◆

If you have fear of cooking fish, try this simple recipe. It's easy and always delivers great flavor, as long as you start with fresh fish. Remember that fresh fish has no "fishy" ammonia odor. It should smell like a fresh ocean breeze. We also make this dish with striped bass, but other fish that have similar medium firm texture and flavor are perch and mahi-mahi. Of course, each fish has its own subtleties and fans. Since this dish is assembled at the last minute, have the greens ready to add to the pan once the fish is cooked.

SHERRY VINAIGRETTE

1 minced shallot

½ teaspoon ground black pepper

3 tablespoons extra virgin olive oil

1 tablespoon sherry vinegar

1 teaspoon chopped fresh oregano

1. In a small bowl whisk all the ingredients together. Reserve.

FISH

1 clove garlic, chopped

1 teaspoon chopped fresh rosemary

1 teaspoon chopped fresh parsley

½ teaspoon fresh ground pepper

2 teaspoons extra virgin olive oil

2 red snapper fillets, about 8 ounces each, approximately ¾ inch thick, boneless and skinless

2 teaspoons canola oil

½ teaspoon kosher salt

1. Place garlic, herbs and pepper on a flat plate. Moisten with the olive oil and mix well.

2. Put the fish, skinned side up, onto the herb mixture and press down. Let it rest in this position for 5 to 10 minutes.

3. Pour the canola oil into a large sauté pan and preheat over medium high until just smoking.

4. Lift the seasoned fish from the plate and sprinkle evenly with kosher salt.

5. Place the fish in the hot pan-seasoned side down, and sear for 3 to 5 minutes. Turn over and sear the other side for an additional 3 to 5 minutes.

6. Remove from the pan and cover to keep warm.

THE GREENS AND TOMATOES

4 grilled roma tomatoes

2 teaspoons olive oil

½ clove garlic, chopped

1 bunch watercress with heavy stems removed

1 head radicchio, root removed and cut into quarters

½ teaspoon salt

2 tablespoons sherry vinaigrette

1. Slice the roma tomatoes in ½-inch-thick slices; brush with olive oil and grill over medium heat, just on one side for about 2 to 3 minutes.

2. Take the hot pan you just cooked the fish in and add the garlic and olive oil. Cook for about half a minute and remove from heat.

3. Add the clean, dry watercress and radicchio to the pan.

4. Drizzle with the sherry vinaigrette, add salt, and toss gently.

5. Divide warmed greens onto plates and top with the seared fish.

6. Garnish with grilled roma tomatoes.

SERVES 2

Flounder with Bananas, Almonds & Rum

◆ ◆ ◆ ◆ ◆

During hurricane season, even Martha's Vineyard has nights of heat and humidity when tropical breezes seem close at hand. Matt created this Black Dog favorite years back when those other islands were beckoning. It remains an oft-requested favorite.

FLOUNDER

1 cup flour
½ teaspoon salt
¼ teaspoon pepper
2 pounds of flounder fillets
2 eggs, beaten
2 tablespoons canola oil
1 tablespoon butter

SAUCE

¼ to ½ cup sliced almonds
2 ripe bananas, sliced
¼ cup rum
2 tablespoons butter
pinch of ground nutmeg
salt & pepper to taste

1. Mix the flour with salt and pepper in a wide, shallow dish.

2. Dredge the flounder in the flour, shake off the excess, and then dip in the beaten egg.

3. Combine the butter and oil in a sauté pan and bring to sizzling hot. Add the flounder fillets and sauté quickly, about two to three minutes per side. Remove from the pan and set aside in a warm oven.

4. To the same pan, add the almonds and sauté briefly, then add the banana slices.

5. Hold the pan away from the heat and add the rum. (Never pour rum or any spirits directly from a bottle into a hot pan, since they are highly flammable.)

6. Return the pan to heat. Add the butter and nutmeg and adjust seasoning. Cook briefly and pour sauce over the flounder.

SERVES 4 TO 6

◆

Flounder Stuffed with Scallop Mousse

◆ ◆ ◆ ◆ ◆

A light dish for an early summer night. Serve with Stir-Fried Sugar Snap Peas, page 186, and crusty bread or roasted new potatoes.

SCALLOP MOUSSE
2 shallots, peeled
1/2 pound scallops, very cold
1/2 cup heavy cream
1 teaspoon chopped parsley
dash nutmeg
salt & pepper

FLOUNDER
butter
8 flounder fillets, about 2 pounds
1/2 cup white wine
juice of 1/2 lemon

1. To prepare the mousse, finely chop the shallots in a food processor. Then add the cold scallops and purée.

2. Slowly add the heavy cream to the puréed scallops. Now add the parsley, nutmeg, salt, and pepper and blend for a few seconds. Reserve.

3. Preheat the oven to 375°F and butter a baking dish. Place a spoonful of the scallop mixture on each flounder fillet. Roll up the fillet and place, seam down, in the baking dish.

4. Pour the wine and lemon juice into the baking dish.

5. Bake for about 10 to 12 minutes. Remove fillets to a warm dish.

6. In a small saucepan, reduce the pan juices by one-third over high heat to concentrate the flavor. Correct the seasoning and spoon over the fillets.

SERVES 4 TO 6

Seared Tuna on Watercress Salad

◆ ◆ ◆ ◆ ◆

The Black Dog is famous for fresh fish, and one reason is Louie Larsen, owner of The Net Result fish market in Vineyard Haven and a member of a multi-generational Island fishing family. Another reason is the relationship The Black Dog and Jack, in particular, have built with the Island fishing fleet over the years. During the season, the day-boats fish about 80 miles out from the Island. Occasionally in late July or August they show up at the dock in front of The Black Dog with whole tuna, freshly caught, and patrons watch our cooks haul a 75-pound fish down the brick walk and into the prep kitchen. We sell a lot of tuna on those days.

1 bunch watercress
3 to 4 red radishes
½ cup jicama
4 to 5 scallions

2 fresh tuna steaks, 8 ounces each
  (approximately 1 inch thick)
1 cup Lemon Sesame Soy Dressing
  (see page 63)

1. Preheat grill.
2. Discard tough fibrous ends of watercress stalks. Wash cress to remove any sand and pat or spin dry.
3. Using a box grater or the shredding blade of a food processor, shred radishes, reserving half of the shredded amount for garnish.
4. Peel the jicama and then shred it also.
5. Prepare the scallions by cutting them crosswise from the root end to the beginning of the dark green section and set aside with the watercress. Cut the dark green ends lengthwise into very thin strips, as long as possible and as thin as patience allows.
6. Plunge the scallion strips into a cup of ice water to form curls. Reserve for garnish.
7. Rub each tuna steak with about one tablespoon of Lemon Sesame Soy Dressing and place on a hot grill. Sear to desired doneness: 1 to 2 minutes per side for rare; 2 to 3 minutes each side for medium and 4 to 6 minutes for well done. We prefer to serve it on the rare side.
8. Toss the watercress in the remaining Lemon Sesame Soy Dressing.
9. For each serving, place dressed salad on the plate with a seared tuna steak on top. Garnish the tuna with the curly scallions and the plate with the reserved shredded radish.

SERVES 2

The Larsen family, with generations of fishing expertise, operate fish markets all over the Island and supply us with the best of the local "bugs," along with lots of other great seafood. You can see Louie Larsen, who runs the Net Result in Vineyard Haven, and his sister Betsy of Larsen's in Menemsha smiling in the sun on this page. The Net Result ships lobsters and lots of other local seafood all over the country. If you'd like to try their fine products, just give them a call. (800 394-6071)

◆ Lobster ◆
THE FUNDAMENTALS

◆ ◆ ◆ ◆ ◆

*L*OBSTERS, OR "BUGS," AS COOKS AND LOBSTERMEN refer to them, have always been a popular item on The Black Dog menu. Most lobster at The Black Dog is served in the traditional way ~ steamed whole with lots of drawn butter for dipping the succulent meat. While just about everyone loves to eat lobster ~ cooking it is another matter. It's the only item on your grocery list that can look you in the eye. Unfortunately, lobster meat spoils very quickly so it is necessary to start with live lobsters and cook them in the most humane manner.

Lobster can be found in sizes from one pound (a/k/a chicken lobster) to up to twenty pounds or more. The most popular size for an individual serving is 1½ pounds. It can be boiled, steamed, baked, grilled or broiled, but it is most commonly boiled or steamed. The other methods require splitting the lobster while still alive, not a fun chore. Research has been done to ascertain the most humane way of cooking lobster, from trying hypnotism to testing the various cooking techniques. The recommendation is to chill lobsters in the refrigerator before cooking in order to "numb" them. This puts them in the slowed state that they naturally have in the winter months. Putting chilled lobsters into a steamer and cooking for 12 to 15 minutes also produces the tenderest meat, since the lobster is less stressed. If you are especially squeamish about cooking lobster, it helps to remember that lobster are carnivores, and will eat each other when given the opportunity. That's why lobsters have their claws banded when you buy them ~ not necessarily to protect your fingers, but to keep the lobsters from attacking each other since they tend to be more cannibalistic when crowded together.

Just Follow These Easy Steps to Steam Lobster for Your Own Feast

◆

1. Choose a 1 to 2 pound lobster per person. Make sure your lobster is fresh; you can keep a lobster under refrigeration safely for twelve hours.
2. Chill the lobsters.
3. Choose a kettle large enough to steam your lobsters. Add approximately one quart of water mixed with 2 tablespoons of salt or use a quart of seawater if it is available. The water should be about 2 inches deep. Use more water if needed.

4. When you have a rolling boil, add the chilled lobsters, cover and steam for 12 to 15 minutes. When the lobster is cooked, it will be red and the antenna will pull out easily.
5. Serve hot with melted butter.

EATING LOBSTER can be a real dining adventure and lots of fun. Make sure that you have nutcrackers, picks and lots of hot steamed towels to pass around at the end of the meal. The easiest method is to start by removing the large claws and setting them aside to crack. Then take the whole lobster in your hands and separate the tail from the body by bending it backwards ~ reversing the tail curl and snapping it off. For beginners, you now have lots of tail and claw meat to enjoy. Those of you who relish the tomalley (the green stuff), sweet legs, and pockets of meat in the carapace don't need further instruction.

◆ Lobster Fra Diavolo ◆

◆ ◆ ◆ ◆ ◆

Those who don't like really hot, spicy food might say this is a hell of a way to treat a lobster ~ but that's the idea. Try this dish if lobster is more than an occasional treat. Choose your favorite pasta to accompany it. We prefer linguine. Note that you should open your kitchen window when sautéeing the hot peppers to avoid burning your eyes.

2 tablespoons extra virgin olive oil
2 teaspoons crushed red pepper
1 minced jalapeño pepper
2 teaspoons chopped garlic
1½ cups Black Dog Sauce (see page 14) or your favorite marinara sauce
2 cooked 1¼-pound lobsters, meat removed and tails split
  (See "Lobster: The Fundamentals," page 149)
1 pound linguine or your favorite pasta

1. In a large, heavy-bottomed sauté pan, heat the oil over medium high heat.

2. Add crushed red pepper and minced jalapeño and cook until the red pepper darkens and the pan is smoking. This must be done in a very well ventilated area because cooking the peppers creates intense fumes that can irritate your eyes.

3. Add the garlic and sauté very quickly, being careful not to burn it. This should only take ten to fifteen seconds.

4. Deglaze the pan with Black Dog Sauce, swirling to pick up all the flavor bits.

5. Add the lobster meat and sauté for 2 to 3 minutes to heat through. Serve over pasta.

SERVES 4

◆ Caramelized Scallops ◆
WITH SMOKED CHILI CREAM

◆ ◆ ◆ ◆ ◆

This procedure works best with large fresh sea scallops, the larger the better! These are great over our Potato Scallion Pancakes (see page 192) or over fresh greens. The delicate sauce adds a zing to sweet scallops. It's also great on grilled fish, enchiladas, or baked potatoes.

SMOKED CHILI CREAM
2 teaspoons chipotle powder
juice of 2 fresh limes
3/4 cup sour cream
salt to taste

1. Mix chipotle powder in lime juice and let it sit and "bloom" for 5 to 10 minutes, then whisk it into sour cream.

2. Add salt to taste. Drizzle over scallops.

YIELDS: 1 CUP

CARAMELIZED SCALLOPS
2 pounds sea scallops
2 tablespoons fresh parsley, chopped
salt and pepper to taste

approximately 1/4 cup extra virgin olive oil
sliced lemons
chopped chives

1. Prepare Smoked Chili Cream first, to allow flavor to develop.

2. On a cutting board, arrange the scallops with flat side down.

3. Sprinkle the top liberally with parsley, salt, and pepper.

4. Heat enough oil to cover the bottom of a large nonstick skillet until oil just begins to smoke.

5. Reduce heat to medium high and place scallops seasoned side down. Do not disturb them for 2 to 3 minutes. This allows the naturally present sugars in the scallop to caramelize.

6. Turn and sear on opposite side for 1 to 3 minutes longer depending on the size of the scallop.

7. Garnish with Smoked Chili Cream, lemons, and chives. Serve immediately.

SERVES 4 TO 6

◆ Bill's Spicy Shrimp ◆
WITH PEPPERS AND ONIONS

◆ ◆ ◆ ◆ ◆

It's often a surprise for summer visitors who call **The Black Dog** about the dinner menu to be told they have to call back about 4:30 p.m. to find out what is being served. That's the time when "the dinner gods" write the list and let the rest of us know what they've been working on since about noon. Every day the menu changes. We see new sauces or fresh veggies just delivered or maybe fish that just became available, but over the decades some entrées have regular repeat performances. Bill's Spicy Shrimp is one of those dishes. We prefer to serve this with fresh Chinese egg noodles. If these are unavailable, substitute the dried variety.

2 tablespoons canola oil
3 teaspoons dark (toasted) sesame oil
3 cloves garlic, chopped
1 tablespoon chopped fresh ginger
16 large shrimp, peeled and deveined
   (see page 96)
8 ounces fresh or dried Chinese egg noodles
1 teaspoon salt

1 green bell pepper, cut into 1-inch squares
1 red bell pepper, cut into 1-inch squares
1 small white onion, diced
1 bunch scallions
1 tablespoon red wine vinegar
3 tablespoons oyster sauce
1 tablespoon dry sherry
1 to 2 teaspoons Tabasco

1. Preheat the canola oil and 1 teaspoon of the sesame oil in a large heavy-bottomed skillet. In a large pot, boil about 6 quarts of water.

2. Add the garlic and ginger to the skillet and sauté until slightly browned. Add the shrimp and sear on one side.

3. Put the Chinese egg noodles in the boiling water. Add salt. If you are using fresh noodles, they will cook in about 3 minutes; dried noodles take about 7 minutes.

4. Turn the shrimp over and add the peppers, onion and scallions. Sauté about 2 minutes.

5. Now add the vinegar, oyster sauce, sherry and Tabasco. Cook about another 2 to 3 minutes. The shrimp should be just done and the veggies should still be crunchy.

6. Toss the drained noodles with the remaining sesame oil.

7. Divide the noodles among plates and top with shrimp and veggies.

SERVES 4 AS AN APPETIZER OR 2 AS AN ENTRÉE

◆

◆ Blackened Shrimp ◆
WITH RED PEPPER COULIS

◆ ◆ ◆ ◆ ◆

Spicy and delicious, this recipe may cause you to restock your spice cabinet but it will be well worth it. A fresh cucumber salad dressed with yogurt and dill would be a good side dish, especially for those who fear the heat.

CHILI RUB
2 tablespoons ancho chili powder
1 teaspoon garlic powder
2 teaspoons onion powder
2 teaspoons ground cumin

1 teaspoon cayenne pepper
2 tablespoons Spanish paprika
1 teaspoon dry marjoram
1 tablespoon kosher salt

RED PEPPER COULIS
3 to 4 large red bell peppers
1 small red onion
1 tablespoon canola oil
1/2 teaspoon crushed red pepper flakes
1 garlic clove, minced

1/2 cup red wine
1/4 cup water
1 tablespoon tomato purée
salt and pepper to taste

SHRIMP
18 to 20 large shrimp
2 to 3 tablespoons of olive oil

GARNISH
sour cream
1/2 cup chopped scallions

TO PREPARE THE CHILI RUB
1. Mix the dry-rub ingredients together in a pie pan and set aside.

TO PREPARE THE COULIS
1. Roast the peppers whole and the onion in quarters under the broiler or on a charcoal grill until the skin blisters on the peppers and the onion wilts.

2. Put the peppers in a paper bag for ten minutes and then peel and seed them. Set aside.

3. Heat the canola oil in a heavy-bottom saucepan over high heat. Add the crushed pepper flakes and heat for a minute to flavor the oil.

4. Add the minced garlic and sauté quickly for about 1 minute. Do not let the garlic burn.

5. Add the onion and roasted pepper. Sauté for 1 minute. Now add the red wine, water, and tomato purée.

6. Continue cooking for about another 3 minutes.

7. Remove from heat and purée this mixture in a blender or food processor, and pass through a fine-holed sieve. Correct seasoning and keep warm.

TO PREPARE THE SHRIMP

1. Peel and devein the shrimp (see "How to Prep Shrimp," page 96).

2. Preheat a heavy-bottomed pan on high. Add the olive oil and heat.

3. Dredge the shrimp in the chili rub and sear in the hot pan on both sides until just done. This should take about two to three minutes maximum per side.

4. Garnish the cooked shrimp with the warm coulis, sour cream, and scallions.

SERVES 2 TO 4

How to Break Down a Chicken

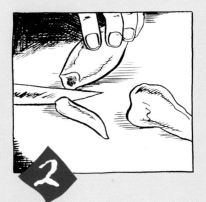

1 Separate a wing from the body and segment at the joint.

2 Cut wing into three sections, reserving tip for stock. Repeat for the other wing.

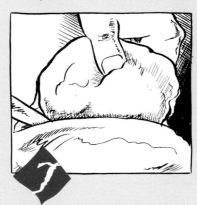

3 Segment the thigh and leg at the ball-and-socket joint.

4 Separate the thigh from leg at the joint.

5 Repeat for the other leg and joint.

6 Cut along breastbone while lifting with finger to remove breast from carcass.

7 Run the knife blade along the rib cage and separate the meat from the bone.

8 The cut chicken parts are ready to use.

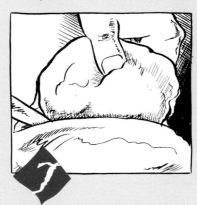

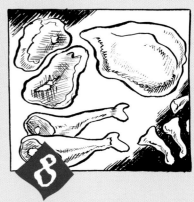

◆ Crunchy Pecan Chicken ◆
WITH LEMON GINGER SAUCE

◆ ◆ ◆ ◆ ◆

Ginger is truly a staple in **The Black Dog** kitchen. We use it to add a fresh-flavored spiciness to a variety of dishes. You'll enjoy the sweet-tart taste of this easily prepared sauce ~ the chicken isn't bad either.

LEMON GINGER SAUCE

juice from 2 lemons
zest from 1/2 lemon
1 tablespoon water

2 tablespoons sugar
1 tablespoon chopped fresh ginger

PECAN CHICKEN

4 skinless, boneless chicken breasts,
  about 8 ounces each
1/2 cup all-purpose flour
1 cup pecan pieces
1/2 cup finely crushed pecans (you
  can do this in a food processor)

1 tablespoon chopped fresh thyme
3/4 teaspoon lemon zest
1/2 teaspoon white pepper
1 teaspoon salt
1 beaten egg
4 to 6 tablespoons canola oil

1. Blend together sauce ingredients and reserve.

2. Lightly pound the chicken breasts to about 1/2-inch thickness.

3. In a shallow dish mix together the flour, pecan pieces, pecan meal, and seasonings. You can use a plastic baggie for this instead of a dish for easy cleanup later.

4. Put the beaten egg in another shallow dish.

5. Preheat the oil in a large, heavy-bottom saucepan on medium-high heat.

6. First drop the chicken breasts in the beaten egg, then remove and dredge in the pecan-flour mixture. Make sure the chicken is evenly coated.

7. Sear the coated chicken in the hot oil until golden brown on each side. This should take about five minutes per side.

8. Serve with Lemon Ginger Sauce.

SERVES 4

◆

Lemon Basil Chicken Piccata with Penne

❖ ❖ ❖ ❖ ❖

Our light, refreshing version of this recipe blends the sweet taste of basil, fresh lemon, and tart capers for a great summer meal. This is a meal that is easily made and always enjoyed.

1 to 1½ pounds penne pasta
1 tablespoon salt
2 chicken breasts, boned and skinned
¼ to ½ teaspoon salt
fresh ground black pepper
2 tablespoons olive oil
2 cloves garlic, chopped

2 teaspoons chopped shallots
2 teaspoons lemon zest
2 to 3 tablespoons fresh lemon juice
½ cup white wine
1 tablespoon capers
1 tablespoon chopped fresh basil
shaved Parmigiano-Reggiano

1. Bring six quarts of water to a boil and add 1 tablespoon of salt.

2. Season chicken breasts with salt and pepper. Make sure they are not thicker than about ¾-inch. Lightly pound if necessary. This ensures that the chicken will cook through in the time allotted.

3. Add dried penne to boiling water and cook for approximately 10 minutes or until al dente. Drain when cooked.

4. While pasta is cooking, heat the oil in a large, heavy-bottomed sauté pan until just smoking. Place chicken breasts in the hot pan.

5. Sear on one side for about 2 to 3 minutes before turning. Then turn over and sear on the other side for about a minute or so.

6. Now add the garlic and shallots to the pan and cook until slightly browned.

7. Add the lemon zest, juice, capers, wine, and basil.

8. Continue to sauté the seasoned chicken for another 3 to 4 minutes until the chicken is thoroughly cooked and all the liquid in the pan has reduced by half.

9. Adjust seasoning and serve over penne. Garnish with shaved cheese.

SERVES 4

◆

Grilled Chicken with
◆ Cilantro Marinade ◆

◆ ◆ ◆ ◆ ◆

Simple is usually best ~ especially on a summer night when the appeal of being outdoors with friends overwhelms any desire to cook. Just mix together your marinade ingredients, spend five or so minutes getting the grill going, and another twenty kicking back ~ this chicken almost cooks itself.

CILANTRO MARINADE
1 to 2 tablespoons chopped fresh cilantro
1 clove of garlic, minced
zest of one lime
2 to 3 tablespoons fresh lime juice
¼ cup extra virgin olive oil
1 teaspoon salt
½ teaspoon black pepper

CHICKEN
4 boned and skinned chicken breasts,
   about 8 ounces each

1. Mix together the marinade ingredients in a deep bowl. Add the chicken breasts and turn to coat completely. Cover the bowl and refrigerate.

2. Marinate for about one hour. You can leave the chicken in the marinade longer, but because this mixture is very acidic, the chicken will begin to appear poached.

3. Preheat your grill. Cook the chicken over medium hot coals for about three to five minutes per side.

4. Serve with Sweet Corn Pepper Salsa, page 115, and warm tortillas.

SERVES 8

Grilled Chicken on
◆ Rosemary Skewers ◆

◆ ◆ ◆ ◆ ◆

This recipe really tempts the senses ~ it's colorful, tasty, and smells especially wonderful as it grills on the rosemary stems. If you have a garden or have access to a garden, acquiring rosemary branches should be easy ~ just choose the woodier branches destined for the pruning pile. Serve with roasted new potatoes or your favorite rice.

MARINADE

½ cup extra virgin olive oil
¼ cup fresh lemon juice
2 cloves garlic, minced
1 tablespoon fresh sage, minced
1 tablespoon fresh oregano, minced

1 tablespoon fresh thyme, minced
¼ cup minced chives
2 teaspoons salt
1 teaspoon fresh ground black pepper

CHICKEN AND VEGGIES

2 to 2½ pounds skinless boneless chicken
(breasts or thighs or both)
1 red bell pepper
1 yellow bell pepper

1 green bell pepper
1 medium yellow onion, cut into 6 wedges
6 large cherry tomatoes
12 medium mushrooms, stems removed

SKEWERS

8 washed, sturdy rosemary branches about 8 to 10 inches long

SEVERAL HOURS BEFORE SERVING

1. In a large glass bowl, mix together the marinade ingredients. Reserve.

2. Cut the chicken pieces into 1½-inch chunks and toss into the marinade.

3. Core, seed, and chop the peppers into 1½-inch pieces and add to the marinade along with the mushroom caps, onion wedges, and cherry tomatoes. Stir this mixture to make sure that the chicken is covered and the veggies have all been coated with the marinade. Cover and refrigerate for several hours.

4. Prepare the skewers by trimming one end into a sharp point and soaking them in water for about an hour before grilling.

GRILLING

1. Preheat the grill to medium-high heat. Drain the chicken and vegetables in a colander, reserving the marinade to use as a basting sauce.

2. For easy "skewering," take a sharp, pointed tool like a metal skewer or meat thermometer and pre-punch each piece of chicken and each veggie.

3. Fill the rosemary branch from base to tip with chicken alternating with veggies. This will keep the rosemary needles flat against the stem. Place a cherry tomato in the center place on each skewer.

4. Place the filled skewers gently on the grill, moving the rack away from the heat if the flames get too high. Don't let the chicken burn. The rosemary skewers will probably char a little at each end.

5. Turn frequently and baste with marinade, being careful not to encourage flare-ups by dripping oil. (When turning with tongs grab the chicken pieces, not the vegetables.)

6. Check for doneness after about 10 to 15 minutes. The chicken should be cooked through but still moist.

SERVES 6 TO 8

◆ Joe's Heel~Proof Chicken ◆

◆ ◆ ◆ ◆ ◆

Cooking on a sailing vessel has its own particular challenges ~ keeping food upright and in the pan is one of them. Deep-frying on the cooktop could be life threatening, so Joe developed this recipe for "just like fried" baked chicken when he was cooking on *Shenandoah*. Unlike the majority of our recipes, this calls for dried herbs and spices, since fresh herbs were rarely, if ever, available in the galley. You can substitute fresh if you have them. The general rule of thumb is that for every teaspoon or tablespoon of dried herbs, you would use three times as much in the fresh state.

½ cup plain bread crumbs
¼ cup all-purpose flour
1 teaspoon salt
½ teaspoon ground
   white pepper
½ teaspoon ground sage
½ teaspoon ground
   marjoram
½ teaspoon thyme leaves
½ teaspoon oregano leaves

½ teaspoon garlic powder
½ teaspoon dried
   minced onion
½ teaspoon ground
   summer savory
½ teaspoon paprika
1 egg, beaten
¼ cup whole milk
2 pounds chicken pieces,
   skin on

1. Preheat oven to 375°F.

2. Combine all the dry ingredients and seasonings in a shallow bowl or heavy-duty plastic bag. Mix together the egg and milk in a bowl.

3. To prepare the chicken, coat each piece thoroughly in the egg mixture first and then in the dry ingredients. This is especially easy if you use a plastic bag for the dry mixture, since you can really shake the chicken pieces around until they are well-coated.

4. Place the chicken pieces in a shallow, non-stick baking dish that is roomy enough so that the chicken pieces do not touch.

5. Bake for about 20 minutes for chicken pieces with bones. Turn the chicken over and continue cooking for an additional 15 minutes or until the chicken is thoroughly cooked. If you decide to use boneless chicken, total cooking time should be about 20 minutes. Make sure to turn the chicken over halfway through the cooking time.

6. Serve with your favorite salad and crusty bread.

SERVES 4 TO 6

◆

*S*HENANDOAH is the seagoing side of The Black Dog family. In years past, Black Dog, our namesake, patrolled her decks as a young pup. Under the steady hand of Captain Robert Douglas, she has spent every summer for more than thirty-five years sailing the warm waters of southern New England. During that time, many of our cooks have spent a few weeks or a season learning to create great food without a lot of fuss or complicated technique on her coal fired stove. Many tavern recipes have evolved from the challenges of feeding hungry sailors three meals a day. Simple, great food ~ that's The Black Dog ~ on land or sea.

MARTHA'S VINEYARD

Coastwise Packet Co.

*S*HENANDOAH

Famous for the love of chickens

Any piece of ground that has been settled since at least the seventeenth century has had its share of unique residents. One of those was nineteenth-century poet and keeper of chickens Nancy Luce. While her poems may not be remembered by a twentieth-century audience, her love of chickens has endured and made her grave a Vineyard landmark.

As they drive up-Island on State Road, past meadows and farms, the sight of large, plastic chickens around her gravestone in the West Tisbury cemetery has caused more than a few drivers to pull up short. Recently the original plastic flock disappeared, but ~ Vineyarders honor their traditions ~ a collection of chicks has taken their place. When you come to the Vineyard, they'll be there keeping Miss Luce company.

◆

◆ Karen's ◆ Tandoori Chicken

◆◆◆◆◆

This dish originates in India, where it is prepared in a "tandoor," a red clay oven. Yogurt tenderizes the chicken and helps the spices to cling to it for better flavor. The lime juice, also a tenderizer, adds tang. Karen developed this recipe at our Bakery Café and suggests drizzling the chicken with yogurt flavored with cilantro, and wrapping it in warm pita bread. We serve it with slices of cucumber or ripe melon.

MARINADE

5 large cloves of garlic
2-inch piece of fresh ginger
½ cup plain lowfat yogurt
1 tablespoon fresh lime juice (about ½ lime)
2 teaspoons salt

1 teaspoon chili powder
1 teaspoon turmeric
½ teaspoon black pepper
½ teaspoon ground cumin
2 teaspoons olive oil

GRILLED CHICKEN

2 pounds boned chicken thighs and breasts
½ cup olive oil

1. In a food processor or mortar, crush the garlic cloves and ginger to make a paste.

2. Put the garlic-ginger paste in a glass bowl or continue in the food processor and add the remaining marinade ingredients and blend well.

3. Add the chicken to the marinade and coat well.

4. Cover and refrigerate for at least two hours to allow the flavors to develop.

5. Get your grill ready. It should be red hot to cook the chicken.

6. Lay the chicken on the grill and baste with the remaining marinade.

7. After about six minutes, turn the chicken and continue cooking for another six to eight minutes.

8. Baste the chicken with olive oil and turn over. Baste with oil again after two to three minutes. When done, the chicken should feel firm.

SERVES 6

◆

Remembering Nancy Luce

Nancy's hens were friends so dear
That even now she keeps them near...
A lasting love that strikes a nerve
In people passing Dead Man's Curve.

~ D.A.W.

◆ Boneless Pork Cutlets ◆
WITH SHALLOT MADEIRA SAUCE

◆ ◆ ◆ ◆ ◆

Serve these as a flavorful alternative to chicken or beef. An easy sauté, it is delicious with roasted corn. Madeira, one of the great flavorful dark sweet wines of Portugal, adds richness to this dish.

COATING MIX

1 cup plain bread crumbs
2 cloves garlic, chopped
¼ cup canola oil

1 tablespoon chopped parsley
1 teaspoon salt
½ teaspoon white pepper

PORK CUTLETS

4 pork cutlets, about 1 to 1¼-inches thick
¼ cup plus 1 tablespoon canola oil
1 clove garlic, chopped
2 tablespoons minced shallots

½ cup Madeira
½ cup chicken stock (see page 44)
salt & pepper to taste

1. Toss together the coating mix ingredients. Once mixed, spread the seasoned crumbs on a large plate.

2. Preheat ¼ cup of oil in a large sauté pan over medium heat.

3. Drizzle the remaining tablespoon of oil on the pork cutlets.

4. Press the oiled pork into the crumb mixture on one side only.

5. Brown the pork nicely on the crumb side. This should take about four minutes in hot oil. Turn to sear on the other side for another three to four minutes.

6. Remove any excess fat and add the garlic and shallots to the cutlets. Sauté for one to two minutes or until slightly browned.

7. Remove pan from heat and add Madeira. Watch out, it may flame. **NOTE**: Make sure when you are adding this, or any liquor, that you pour it from a measuring cup, **NOT** the bottle.

8. Return the pan to heat and cook for about one minute, stirring and blending to deglaze the pan and scrape up all the bits that have stuck to it. Now add the stock and continue cooking until the liquid is reduced by half. Season with salt and pepper.

9. Place the cooked pork on serving plates and drizzle with the Madeira reduction.

SERVES 2 TO 4

◆

◆ Grilled Pork Cutlets ◆
WITH MAPLE CHIPOTLE GLAZE

◆ ◆ ◆ ◆ ◆

This spicy smoky glaze is great on quick-cooking cutlets, and if you have more time, try it on ribs or roast a whole pork loin.

MAPLE GLAZE
½ cup maple syrup
½ cup chicken stock
  (see page 44)
1½ teaspoons chipotle powder
1 teaspoon fresh thyme, chopped
2 teaspoons cornstarch
1 tablespoon water, cold

PORK CUTLETS
1½ pounds pork cutlets,
   cut ¾ inch thick
salt & pepper
1 tablespoon canola oil

1. Preheat your grill. In a small saucepan, bring the first four glaze ingredients to a boil.

2. In a small jar mix together the cornstarch and water. Put the lid on and shake vigorously. This is an easy way to make sure the slurry combines. It should have the consistency of whole milk.

3. Pour the cornstarch slurry into the boiling glaze mixture and reduce to a simmer. Cook about two minutes until it becomes clear and thickens.

4. Season the cutlets with salt and pepper and brush with a little oil.

5. Grill cutlets 3 to 5 minutes per side, brushing the glaze on while cooking.

SERVES 6

◆

◆ Grilled Lamb Kabobs ◆

◆◆◆◆◆

This recipe comes down from Bill Prokos and Lucia Moffett, who operated Helios, a restaurant that began as a tiny take-out stand in Edgartown. It moved later to a building that James Taylor owned. Bill and Lucia were famous for their lamb kabobs and appeared as guest chefs at The Black Dog in the early days. Their version of "Greek Night" at the Tavern was always a wild success ~ bazouki music blaring and lines of dancing customers and crew, fueled by "bring your own ouzo." Occasionally Bill would exuberantly demonstrate how to dance with a table in your teeth or the proper way to throw dinner plates into the fireplace. You don't have to do any of that to enjoy this dish ~ but wouldn't it be fun!

½ cup extra virgin olive oil,
   preferably Greek
¼ cup lemon juice
3 to 5 cloves garlic, thinly sliced
1 teaspoon salt
1 tablespoon lemon zest
3 tablespoons fresh oregano, minced
3 tablespoons fresh rosemary, chopped
1 tablespoon fresh mint, minced
1 bay leaf

freshly ground pepper
2½ pounds boneless leg of lamb,
   cut into cubes
1 red bell pepper, cut in wedges
1 green bell pepper, cut in wedges
12 fresh mushroom caps (or cherry tomatoes)
2 medium red onions, cut in wedges
wood skewers, 12 inches or longer
   (soaked in water) or metal skewers

1. In a large non-reactive bowl, whisk together the olive oil, lemon juice, garlic and salt.

2. Add the herbs and lemon zest. Blend well.

3. Put the lamb cubes and onion wedges into the marinade. Toss well to coat completely with marinade and cover. Refrigerate for several hours, or better yet, overnight.

4. Prepare the grill and bring to medium high heat. If you are using wooden skewers soak them well to prevent burning.

5. Remove the lamb and onions from the marinade, reserving liquid. Discard bay leaf.

6. Prepare kabobs by alternating cubes of lamb with pepper and onion wedges and as many mushroom caps or tomatoes as you like on the wooden or metal skewers. Lay the prepared skewers in a shallow dish and brush with reserved marinade.

7. Grill over medium hot coals for about 8 to 10 minutes until the lamb is just medium rare, turning the skewers several times for even cooking.

SERVES 6

◆ Grilled Butterflied Leg of Lamb ◆

◆ ◆ ◆ ◆ ◆

Served medium rare with a little char crust from the fire, butterflied leg of lamb is delicious. Just follow Joe's easy recipe ~ he knows his lamb; back before The Black Dog became the focus of his attention, he worked at Helios, where lamb was a specialty and he grilled more than 60 pounds of lamb there a day.

½ cup olive oil
¼ cup good red wine vinegar
6 garlic cloves, minced
½ cup chopped fresh rosemary or a combination of fresh rosemary, thyme and oregano
1 boned leg of lamb, 5 to 6 pounds (Have your butcher trim the fat and butterfly it for you.
  You can substitute a boneless shoulder, but marinate it longer.)
1 teaspoon salt
1 teaspoon fresh ground pepper

1. Mix together the oil, vinegar, garlic, and herbs in a large glass pan. Add the lamb and sprinkle with salt and pepper.

2. Turn the lamb several times in the marinade mixture to coat thoroughly. Cover and refrigerate for several hours; overnight is best. Make sure to turn the lamb occasionally. The key to this recipe is allowing time for the lamb to marinate. Prepare your grill.

3. Remove the lamb from the marinade, reserving the marinade mixture.

4. Grill over medium-hot coals, flat skin side first, for about 8 minutes. Then turn it often after that. You may brush the remaining marinade on the lamb as it cooks, but watch out for flare-ups. You don't want the meat too charred. The meat should be just rare to medium rare at the thickest, chunkiest part, and the thinner sections should be medium rare to medium after grilling for 25 to 30 minutes.

5. Once grilled to desired doneness, remove the lamb and let it rest for at least 5 minutes before slicing it as shown. We serve it with Moroccan Cous Cous, page 78.

SERVES 8

◆

Lamb Chops with Juniper Berry Marinade

◆ ◆ ◆ ◆ ◆

Summer is about cooking outdoors whenever you have the chance. This classic combination of garlic, lamb, and rosemary with the extra kick of juniper berries makes a great grilled meal. Serve with the Beet, Orange, and Feta Salad on page 65, and a loaf of crusty bread.

¼ cup lemon juice
¼ cup red wine
¼ cup olive oil
2 garlic cloves, sliced

1 teaspoon salt
1 tablespoon crushed juniper berries
1 tablespoon chopped fresh rosemary
4 loin lamb chops, about 1 to 1½-inch thick

1. Assemble the marinade ingredients in a shallow dish, small enough to allow the lamb chops to steep in the marinade.

2. Marinate the lamb for two to four hours.

3. Prepare your grill. Grill the chops, basting a few times with the marinade, to your preferred level of doneness, about 7 minutes per side for medium.

SERVES 4

Spicy Grilled Tenderloin of Beef
WITH GRILLED VEGETABLE SALSA

◆ ◆ ◆ ◆ ◆

GRILLED TENDERLOIN

1 tablespoon each: cumin seed, coriander
   seed, fennel seed, crushed red and ground
   black pepper, dried oregano, dried basil
¼ cup coarse salt
½ cup olive oil
6 trimmed 8-ounce tenderloin steaks

1. Put the cumin, coriander, and fennel
   seeds in a dry, hot skillet to toast. Keep
   them moving around the pan until they
   start to smoke, but not burn, then remove
   them from the heat and let them cool.
   Toasting the seeds increases the pungency
   of these spices.

2. After they have cooled off, put all the
   seeds and the herbs into a spice or food
   mill for about four to five seconds to
   crush but not pulverize them.

3. In a mixing bowl combine the crushed
   spices and the coarse salt.

4. Pat the steaks dry and coat them with the
   olive oil and then cover with the
   spice/salt mixture. Let stand at room
   temperature, covered, for at least an hour,
   or refrigerate overnight, to absorb the
   flavors.

5. Get your grill ready and prepare the
   Grilled Vegetable Salsa.

6. Bring your beef to room temperature
   before grilling. The steaks should take
   about five to eight minutes for rare to
   medium rare. Turn to prevent burning.

7. Cut in ¾-inch slices and serve with
   Grilled Vegetable Salsa, opposite.

SERVES 6

GRILLED VEGETABLE SALSA

1 sweet onion, in large slices
1 yellow pepper, whole
1 poblano pepper, whole
1 jalapeño pepper, whole
3 ripe tomatoes, whole
juice of two limes
¼ cup chopped fresh cilantro
½ cup olive oil
2 teaspoons salt
1 teaspoon ground white pepper

1. Coat the vegetables with some of the oil and grill for about five minutes, turning once.

2. Peel and seed tomatoes and peppers. Take care when peeling and seeding the jalapeño pepper ~ its oil can burn your face and especially your eyes.

3. Place all of the ingredients in a food processor and chop into a coarse mixture.

4. Remove and place in a bowl and let stand for about fifteen minutes.

◆ Beef Teriyaki ◆

◆ ◆ ◆ ◆ ◆

Teriyaki-style beef has a sweet-salty taste. This dish can be done on a charcoal fire, gas grill, or in your oven broiler. Serve with rice or noodles and a few sautéed seasonal vegetables.

¾ cup tamari
¾ cup sake
¼ cup sugar
3 tablespoons canola oil
2 teaspoons dark sesame oil

1 tablespoon minced fresh ginger
3 cloves garlic, minced
2 pounds sirloin tips or skirt steak
bamboo skewers soaked in water

1. To prepare the marinade, mix all of the ingredients except the beef in a medium-size bowl.

2. Slice the beef against the grain in long, thin strips. This is much easier to do if the beef is put into the freezer until nearly frozen.

3. Marinate the beef strips for about two hours.

4. Remove the beef from the marinade and thread it on the bamboo skewers.

5. Put the marinade in a small saucepan and cook over medium heat to reduce and thicken, about 5 to 7 minutes. Stir frequently to prevent burning.

6. Grill over hot coals (the best method), gas grill, or in the broiler for about five minutes a side, basting frequently with the reduced marinade mixture.

7. To serve, pour the reduced marinade over the beef to coat.

SERVES 6 TO 8

◆ Sirloin Tips Quasimodo ◆

◆ ◆ ◆ ◆ ◆

What is it? Quasi aioli, but more than just a garlic mayonnaise. Quasi moutarde, but with lots of extras. That's why we call it Quasimodo ~ to indicate its hidden qualities. (Victor Hugo has nothing to do with it.) We use it with lots of different grilled meats, but perhaps our long-term favorite is as an accompaniment to sirloin tips. Cut back on the garlic if your tolerance is low, and take the time to find Pommery mustard if it's not already on your refrigerator shelf. It has whole mustard seeds and a strong vinegar bite.

QUASIMODO SAUCE
5 to 7 chopped garlic cloves
1 egg yolk
½ teaspoon Dijon mustard
1 tablespoon Pommery mustard
1 tablespoon horseradish
pinch of salt
pinch of ground white pepper
2 tablespoons red wine vinegar
1½ cups extra virgin olive oil

1. In a food processor, combine the chopped garlic, egg yolk, mustards, horseradish, salt, pepper and vinegar. Blend well.

2. With the processor running, add the olive oil in a thin stream. It should emulsify to a mayonnaise-like consistency.

3. Chill until ready to use. This makes about 1½ cups and will keep about 2 weeks under refrigeration.

SIRLOIN TIPS
1½ to 2 pounds of sirloin tips or strip steak
salt & pepper

1. Season the steak with salt and pepper and grill over coals or on a gas grill to desired doneness. A good rule of thumb for a 1-inch-thick sirloin is 4 to 5 minutes per side for medium rare.

2. Cut the meat across the grain in ½-inch slices.

3. Serve with Quasimodo Sauce and your choice of veggies.

SERVES 6 TO 8

◆

◆ Cowboy Ribeye Steak ◆

◆ ◆ ◆ ◆ ◆

When you really want to sit down to a great steak dinner, here's our pick ~ great sauce, tasty peppers, easy cooking. What could be bad?

SWEET & SMOKY BARBECUE SAUCE

2 teaspoons canola oil
1 small white onion, minced
2 cloves garlic, chopped
1 cup ketchup

3 tablespoons brown sugar
1/4 cup white vinegar
1 tablespoon Worcestershire sauce
2 teaspoons chipotle powder

1. Place a small saucepan over medium heat. Add the oil.

2. Place the onion and the garlic in the hot oil and cook until they sizzle.

3. Now add the remaining ingredients to the pan and reduce to a simmer. Cook for about 5 minutes.

4. Keep warm.

PEPPER & ONION SAUTÉ

1 medium white onion, preferably Vidalia
1 medium green bell pepper
1 medium red bell pepper
2 teaspoons canola oil

1. Seed the peppers and slice into 1/4-inch strips. Slice the onion into 1/4-inch rings.

2. Preheat a sauté pan and add the oil.

3. Add the onion and cook until translucent, about 2 to 3 minutes.

4. Add the peppers and continue cooking another 2 to 3 minutes, until the peppers are soft.

5. Keep warm.

STEAKS

4 boneless ribeye steaks, about 1-inch thick

1. Grill the steaks over hot coals to your desired doneness. Baste frequently with the sauce.

2. Approximate grilling times for 1-inch-thick steak: 2 to 3 minutes per side for rare; 3 to 4 minutes per side for medium rare; 4 to 5 minutes per side for medium to medium well; 6 to 7 minutes per side for well done.

3. Serve topped with pepper & onion sauté.

SERVES 4

◆ Porterhouse Steaks ◆
WITH CRACKED BLACK PEPPERCORNS

◆ ◆ ◆ ◆ ◆

In eighteenth-century English taverns, those responsible for the well-being of the occupants were called "porters." As the story goes, these porters were known to consume large quantities of ale ~ apparently taking good care of their own well-being. Eventually a place that served drink was known as a "porterhouse" and these establishments also served good cuts of beef. The porterhouse steak was made famous way back when by the proprietor of an old New York "porterhouse." A combination of the tenderest beef on one side of the bone and the most flavorful on the other side, this is a good cut for broiling or grilling as well as sautéeing.

¼ cup whole black peppercorns
4 porterhouse steaks, about 20 ounces each and about 1½ inches thick
salt to taste
1 cup hearty red wine
2 tablespoons butter

1. Place a small amount of the peppercorns in the middle of a large hard cutting board. Take a heavy, smooth-bottomed pan firmly in both hands and mash the peppercorns under the pan with a rolling motion from one side to the other. Repeat until all the peppercorns are cracked coarsely.

2. Trim any excess fat from the edges of the steaks and reserve a few small pieces.

3. Evenly sprinkle the crushed peppercorns on each side of the steaks, pressing them into the steak's surface.

4. Put two cast-iron skillets or heavy sauté pans on medium heat and render the reserved fat in each so that you have about 1 tablespoon of grease in each pan, thoroughly coating the bottom. Heat until just smoking.

5. Place the steaks in the pan with the tenderloin side farthest away from the heat and sear for 2 to 3 minutes.

6. Turn over and sear for about the same amount of time on the other side. Don't be afraid to move the steaks around in the pan.

7. Continue cooking and turning for about 10 minutes until the steaks are medium rare. Check frequently ~ it takes a much shorter time to go from rare to well done than it takes to go from raw to rare.

8. Remove steaks when done to your liking and keep warm. Deglaze the pan with the red wine and reduce. Whisk in the butter when the wine has reduced by half. Pour over steaks and serve.

SERVES 6 TO 8

Southwestern Rubbed Strip Steak

◆ ◆ ◆ ◆ ◆

Dry rubs ~ mixtures of salt and ground herbs and spices ~ not only add flavor to your meats, they also enhance its moisture by helping to seal in the meat juices. We've chosen strip steak for this recipe, but you can substitute another favorite cut. This rub is also great on pork.

2 tablespoons ancho chili powder
1 teaspoon garlic powder
2 teaspoons onion powder
2 teaspoons ground cumin
1 teaspoon cayenne pepper
2 tablespoons Spanish paprika
1 teaspoon dried thyme
1 teaspoon dry marjoram
1 tablespoon kosher salt
2 twelve-ounce strip steaks

Horses always start, they never run out of gas and they will not get you greasy.

~ GLADIOLA MONTANA

1. Mix dry ingredients together in a pie pan.

2. Dry two twelve-ounce strip steaks and lay them in the pie pan to coat both sides of the steaks with the rub mixture.

3. Broil or grill to desired level of doneness, usually about 4 to 5 minutes a side for medium rare. If Ancho chili powder is unavailable locally, you can make your own by grinding whole Ancho chilis (dry poblano) in your food processor. We serve this at The Black Dog with Mashed Sweet Potatoes with Lime & Chipotle (see recipe on page 185.)

SERVES 4 TO 6

◆

Vegetables

Mashed Sweet Potatoes with Lime & Chipotle

◆ ◆ ◆ ◆ ◆

You many not have heard of chipotle peppers but you know their original incarnation ~ jalapeños. Smoked and dried and renamed, these peppers add a delicious rich flavor of smoke and earth. Not too spicy, just good!

4 large sweet potatoes, approximately 2 pounds
3 tablespoons butter
1 teaspoon chipotle powder
juice from one fresh lime
½ teaspoon salt

1. Peel the sweet potatoes and cut into 2-inch cubes.

2. Steam over about 2 inches of boiling water until soft, about 15 minutes. We prefer this method to boiling, as it seems to retain more flavor.

3. In a small saucepan, melt the butter; whisk in the chipotle powder, salt, and fresh lime juice.

4. Pour this mixture over the hot steamed potatoes.

5. With a potato masher or electric mixer on slow speed, blend until the sweet potato mixture is smooth.

SERVES 4 TO 6

◆ Stir~Fried Sugar Snap Peas ◆

Fast and delicious, this is a great way to cook these sweet tasty vegetables. Remember, you want to keep the snap in these peas, so don't overcook them.

½ pound fresh sugar snap peas
2 tablespoons vegetable oil
1 teaspoon dark sesame oil
3 tablespoons pinenuts

1 tablespoon minced fresh ginger
2 tablespoons dry sherry
2 tablespoons tamari

1. To prepare sugar snaps, snap off the stem and pull the fibrous string off along the seam.

2. Heat a wok or heavy skillet over high heat. Pour in the vegetable oil and once it is hot, add the sesame oil.

3. Add the pinenuts and ginger to the hot oil and stir-fry to brown the pinenuts, being careful not to burn them.

4. Now add the snap peas and stir-fry to coat with the oil. Mix in the sherry and tamari, cover the wok and lower the heat to medium. Cook for about two minutes to cook the peas through but still keep the snap.

5. Serve family style or over rice for a light vegetarian meal.

SERVES 4 AS A SIDE DISH

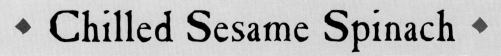

◆ Chilled Sesame Spinach ◆

Not from Popeye's era, this up-to-date, Asian-influenced chilled spinach side dish is full of savory flavor. Easy to make, just plan ahead to allow for chillin' time. We serve it cold with Sesame Crusted Salmon, page 131.

1 package fresh spinach, about 10 ounces
1½ to 2 tablespoons dark sesame oil
¼ teaspoon crushed red pepper flakes

2 garlic cloves, chopped
2 teaspoons sesame seeds
pinch of salt

1. Rinse the spinach well. Pick over and discard any tough leaves and stems. Dry and reserve.

2. Place a sauté pan over medium heat and add the sesame oil and crushed red pepper flakes. Heat.

3. Add the garlic and sesame seeds and sauté until both are slightly browned.

4. Now add the cleaned spinach and cook, stirring frequently to mix in the garlic and sesame seeds. Watch carefully and remove from heat when just wilted. Season with salt.

5. Put the wilted spinach in a colander to drain and chill for about an hour.

SERVES 2 GENEROUSLY

◆ Grilled Sesame Hijiki ◆

◆ ◆ ◆ ◆ ◆

This cold salad made with a calcium-rich seaweed called hijiki offers an interesting and tasty change from more traditional shredded salads like cole slaw. Hand-harvested in the wild, where it grows on rocky ledges, this sea veggie is washed, steamed, and sun-dried before packaging. Tossed together with crunchy jicama and peppers, it makes a great accompaniment to grilled meats and fish.

1 cup dried hijiki (2-ounce package)
4 red radishes
1 medium carrot
1 small red onion
¼ pound jicama
1 small red bell pepper
1 small yellow bell pepper

1 small poblano pepper
½ bunch scallions
1 tablespoon white sesame seeds
¼ cup toasted sesame oil
⅓ cup rice wine vinegar
¼ cup tamari

1. Cover the dried hijiki with two cups of cold water and let it stand for 45 minutes to an hour to soften and rehydrate. Drain off the excess water.

2. Prepare the radishes, carrot, onion, jicama, peppers, and scallions by cutting into strips of matchstick size. You can use the shredding blade of your food processor if you choose, but we prefer handcutting to retain better texture and the individual flavors of each vegetable.

3. In small dry, non-stick pan toast the sesame seeds over medium heat. Do not burn.

4. Put the prepared veggies in a medium-size bowl and toss with the toasted seeds, oil, vinegar, and tamari.

5. Add the rehydrated hijiki strips and mix well to thoroughly coat and blend.

6. Refrigerate overnight for better flavor. You can keep this mixture for up to one week under refrigeration.

YIELDS: ABOUT 4 CUPS

◆

Orzo with Feta, Spinach & Tomatoes

◆ ◆ ◆ ◆ ◆

Pasta salad Greek-style, this dish features orzo, which looks like rice but is, in fact, traditional Greek pasta. Toss it hot with feta cheese and spinach and a few pinenuts for a great side dish, or serve it cold with additional oil and vinegar to your taste. It's great with Lamb Kabobs, page 171.

2 tablespoons olive oil
1/3 cup pinenuts
1/4 teaspoon salt
2 tablespoons balsamic vinegar
1 clove garlic, minced
1 cup tender spinach leaves,
    stemmed and coarsely chopped
1/4 cup Italian parsley, coarsely chopped
1 cup tomatoes, chopped
    (and peeled, if you like)
1 tablespoon grated lemon zest
1/3 pound feta, drained and crumbled
1 1/2 cups (12 ounces) orzo
salt and pepper to taste

1. Heat 1 tablespoon of the olive oil in a sauté pan until hot and add pinenuts. Sauté, tossing or stirring frequently, until lightly browned. Sprinkle with salt while sautéing. This should take about 2 or 3 minutes. Remove from pan and drain pinenuts on paper towels.

2. In a medium-size bowl whisk the remaining tablespoon of olive oil with the vinegar and garlic. Add the spinach, parsley, tomatoes, lemon zest, and feta and toss together gently.

3. Bring 2 quarts of water to a boil; add salt and the orzo. Stir occasionally and cook until al dente, about 12 minutes.

4. Drain the hot orzo and rinse under running water briefly. Drain. Add the still-hot orzo to the feta and spinach mixture. Toss lightly, add salt and pepper to taste and sprinkle with pinenuts.

SERVES 4

◆

◆ Stir~Fried Zucchini ◆
WITH SPICY PEANUT SAUCE

◆ ◆ ◆ ◆ ◆

If your summer garden includes zucchini, here's a recipe that will make you want to plant more of that bountiful vegetable.

COOKING SAUCE

3 tablespoons tahini, well blended
3 tablespoons hot water
3 tablespoons tamari

3 tablespoons vegetable oil
2 teaspoons sugar
2 teaspoons rice wine vinegar

STIR-FRY INGREDIENTS

2 tablespoons vegetable oil
2 teaspoons dark (toasted) sesame oil
½ cup shelled raw peanuts
2 tablespoons chili paste
5 cloves garlic, chopped

6 small to medium zucchini, quartered lengthwise, then cut into 2-inch spears
3 tablespoons dry sherry
5 scallions, sliced, for garnish

1. To prepare the cooking sauce, whisk together the tahini and hot water in a small bowl. Add the tamari and remaining cooking sauce ingredients one at a time, blending the mixture until smooth after each one. Set aside.

2. Heat the vegetable oil in a wok or heavy skillet until smoking hot. Add the dark sesame oil. Quickly add the peanuts and stir them continually to brown without burning. Next add the chili paste and garlic and stir briefly to heat through.

3. Add the zucchini spears and stir-fry for a minute or two to heat through. Add the sherry and continue cooking as the sherry reduces. This should take about a minute.

4. Add the cooking sauce and lower the heat to medium. Cook for another minute or so.

5. Serve family style, garnished with the sliced scallions.

SERVES 4 TO 6 AS A SIDE DISH

◆ Potato Scallion Pancakes ◆

◆ ◆ ◆ ◆ ◆

At The Black Dog we serve these potato pancakes with our Caramelized Scallops (see page 153) as an unusual side dish. Choose them to accompany grilled pork chops or other grilled meats. Just top them with minced chives and parsley and serve with sour cream on the side.

1½ pounds red bliss potatoes, scrubbed
1 bunch scallions cut into ¼-inch slices
½ cup or so of all-purpose flour
2 beaten eggs

1 teaspoon salt
½ teaspoon white pepper
4 tablespoons canola or olive oil

1. Shred the unpeeled potatoes in a food processor or with a box grater. Make sure to drain the shredded potatoes well. It's sometimes necessary to squeeze the shredded potatoes between two clean dishtowels to remove extra moisture. You want to start with dry potatoes.

2. In a large bowl mix together the shredded potatoes, scallions, flour, eggs, and seasonings until evenly blended. Do not overmix. Covering with plastic wrap right on the potato mix will help to avoid discoloration.

3. Heat 1 tablespoon of oil in an 8-inch non-stick pan over medium-high heat. Place ¼ of the mixture in the hot pan and allow to set for 2 to 3 minutes. Do not let it burn. Turn over and cook on the other side. The pancake should be golden brown. If you prefer smaller pancakes, reduce amount of potato mixture.

4. Continue this procedure, adding more oil as necessary, until all the pancakes are cooked. Hold in a warm oven until ready to serve.

SERVES 4 TO 6

◆  ◆

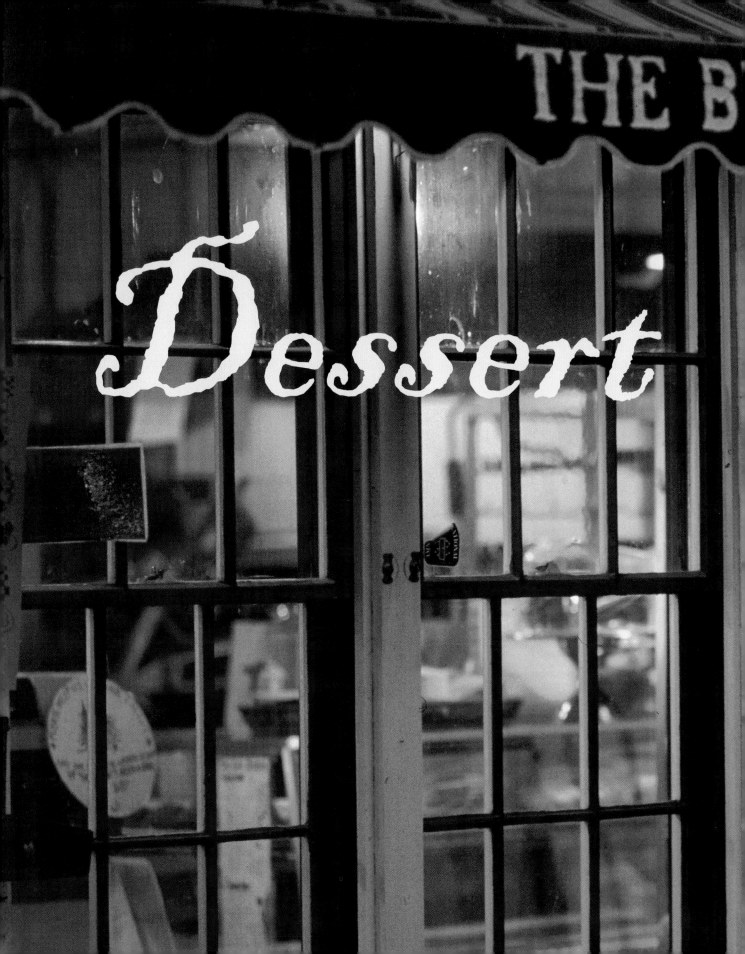

WITH SHELVES full of hearth bread and cases full of pastries, chewies, and other delectables, The Black Dog Bakery has been offering delicious ways to expand the waistline for nearly thirty years. No wonder it's often the last stop on the way to the ferry for Islanders and visitors alike. All of our bakery treats are made from scratch, with one surprising exception (see **Fudge Bottom Pie**), using the best ingredients such as fresh eggs, butter, pure flavorings and the finest chocolate. Here are just a few of our favorites to tempt you ~ there's a Black Dog Bakery cookbook in our future.

◆ Fudge Bottom Pie ◆

◆ ◆ ◆ ◆ ◆

For more than twenty years, this popular dessert has stayed on The Black Dog menu. As our pastry chefs have become more skilled we've tried to change it or remove it and replace it, but our patrons won't put up with that nonsense. We've had people call to let us know they were coming in just for Fudge Bottom, or as we affectionately refer to it, "fun with Jell-O." Nothing short of buying dessert could be easier than making this recipe, and kids love it. The freezing process stabilizes the filling; it slices best when it is semi-frozen. So cut it that way at the beginning of your meal and it should be thawed but still cold by dessert time.

GRAHAM CRACKER CRUST

1 cup graham cracker crumbs
⅛ cup confectioners' sugar
2½ tablespoons unsalted butter

1. Mix sugar and graham cracker crumbs together in a bowl.

2. Melt the butter and pour it little by little onto the crumb mixture. Incorporate by kneading with your fingertips.

3. Press into a 9-inch pie plate and freeze until needed.

CHOCOLATE GANACHE

½ pound dark chocolate (we use Callebaut bittersweet couverture)
½ pint heavy cream

1. Finely chop the chocolate and place into a medium-size stainless-steel bowl.

2. Pour the cream into a small saucepan and place over a medium-high flame until scalded (slightly bubbling) but not boiling. Watch this: it only takes a few minutes.

3. Carefully pour the cream over the chocolate and let it sit for about 5 minutes. Then whisk the mixture until the cream is completely incorporated. The chocolate should be smooth with no lumps.

4. Cool slightly and use immediately or cool completely, wrap, and refrigerate for up to a week. You can reheat ganache by putting it in a double boiler over medium heat, stirring occasionally until completely melted and smooth.

FILLING

2 boxes of Jell-O instant vanilla pudding mix, 3.4-ounce size
1 pint cold heavy cream
1 pint cold light cream

1. Pour the light cream and heavy cream into a large mixing bowl. Add the dry pudding mix. Whip on high speed until firm peaks form.

PIE

1. Pour the melted chocolate ganache evenly into the frozen graham cracker crust and chill until the ganache is completely set and firm. This takes about 1 to 1½ hours.

2. Spoon the filling into the pie pan over the frozen ganache and swirl the top in a spiral fashion to form a voluptuous peak.

3. Garnish with cocoa or chocolate shavings and freeze uncovered for 4 to 5 hours, until completely frozen. If prolonged freezing is more convenient, wrap the frozen pie tightly with plastic wrap to avoid freezer burn.

4. Semi-thaw in the refrigerator to slice. Thaw slices completely to serve.

SERVES 6 TO 8

◆ Blackout Cake ◆

◆ ◆ ◆ ◆ ◆

This recipe makes a delicious, moist chocolate cake without eggs. Because the frosting recipe requires an hour of refrigeration, make the frosting first. If you don't have much time, it's also great without frosting, just dust with some confectioners' sugar. There's more than one story to explain its name. Our version is that this cake is so rich, you could just faint from overindulgence.

FROSTING

1½ cups sugar
1 cup unsweetened cocoa powder
1 cup heavy cream

1 tablespoon honey
2 tablespoons butter
1 tablespoon pure vanilla extract

1. Sift together the sugar and cocoa powder and set aside.

2. In a saucepan over medium heat, mix the heavy cream with the honey, butter, and vanilla. Add the sugar and cocoa and stir the mixture with a whisk for 8 to 10 minutes until completely smooth. Do not allow to boil.

3. Remove from heat. Cover and cool the frosting for an hour in the refrigerator. Before using, whip with a hand-held mixer at medium speed until light and fluffy.

CAKE

2 cups sugar
2 teaspoons baking soda
1 teaspoon salt
6 tablespoons unsweetened cocoa powder
3 cups cake flour

¾ cup canola oil
2 tablespoons white vinegar
2 cups cold water
confectioners' sugar for dusting finished cake

1. Preheat oven to 350°F and prepare two 9-inch round cake pans, at least 2½ inches deep, with butter, oil, or parchment paper ~ your preference. We prefer to oil the pans and add parchment paper circles to the bottom.

2. Sift together dry ingredients and place in a large bowl. Mix all wet ingredients together and pour into the dry. Combine well with a whisk or mixer until batter is smooth.

3. Pour into two prepared baking pans and bake for approximately 20 minutes.

4. Cool completely on a rack. Trim the cakes to stand about 1½ inches tall. Cut trimmed-off tops into ½ to 1 inch cubes and set aside. To frost, place one layer on a plate and spread ⅓ of the frosting on it. Top with the second layer and spread remaining frosting on top and sides. Press the cake cubes all over the top and sides, into the frosting. Distribute as evenly as possible. You now have a "bumpy" cake.

5. Dust with confectioners' sugar and serve.

SERVES 8 TO 10

Whipped Cream

BLACK DOG WAITRONS WHIP a lot of cream and often do it in warm weather. The secret is to keep everything cold and use a big balloon whisk. Just take two stainless steel bowls and fill one with ice. Nest the other bowl inside where it will stay really cold and pour in cold heavy cream. If you want about 2 cups of whipped cream, use ½ pint of heavy cream.

GET THAT WHISK GOING. Whipping cream takes a few minutes, and your arm will get a bit of a workout, but think of the calories you'll burn. (You may use a portable mixer if you prefer.) When the cream forms light soft peaks, stop ~ overbeaten cream becomes butter eventually. It will start looking grainy and break up if you whip it too much. This happened to us twice while we were doing the photo shoot for this cookbook. If you want to add sugar or flavoring like vanilla or almond extract or any liquor, wait until the cream is whipped and fold the flavoring in gently.

One delicious taste treat that takes a simple dessert to another level of delight is whipped cream. Just put some on a brownie, a slice of cake, or some fresh berries ~ and you have a celebration. It's always on hand at The Black Dog ~ for Belgian waffles in the morning and pie at night.

◆ Black Dog Ginger Cookies ◆

◆ ◆ ◆ ◆ ◆

People have been known to stand in line at **The Black Dog Bakery** for these cookies. This recipe makes a lot, so you'll have plenty of delicious treats to show for your effort ~ good keepers and great for a bake sale! **Note**, remember to reserve 1 cup of sugar to roll the finished balls of cookie dough in before baking.

½ cup coarsely chopped fresh ginger
1½ cups canola oil
3 cups granulated sugar, plus 1 cup for
   rolling dropped cookie dough
¾ cup molasses
3 eggs
1½ teaspoons salt
1 tablespoon cinnamon
5¼ teaspoons baking soda
¾ teaspoon ground cloves
7 cups pastry flour

1. Preheat oven to 350°F.

2. Mix the fresh ginger with one-half cup of the oil in a food processor until well-minced.

3. In a large mixing bowl blend 3 cups of the sugar, molasses and eggs.

4. Strain the minced ginger/oil mixture, reserving the liquid. Add this liquid, plus the remaining cup of oil to the egg mixture and blend until smooth.

5. In a separate bowl mix together the salt, cinnamon, baking soda, cloves, and flour.

6. Add the dry mix to the wet mix and blend well.

7. Either line your cookie sheets with parchment paper, or grease with butter.

8. Scoop the cookie dough by teaspoonfuls and roll in the reserved cup of granulated sugar.

9. Place on prepared cookie sheets and bake for about eight to twelve minutes, just until the tops crack and the cookies are flat.

10. Cool completely on wire racks. Enjoy!

MAKES ABOUT EIGHT DOZEN COOKIES

◆

Sue's Luscious Lemon Squares

◆ ◆ ◆ ◆ ◆

On a warm summer day, Sue's cool and tart squares are the perfect dessert. This recipe makes at least twenty-four, depending on how you cut them. Bring them to your next family gathering!

CRUST
3/4 pound cold unsalted butter
3 cups unbleached flour
3/4 cup confectioners' sugar

TOPPING
1/2 cup sifted confectioners' sugar

FILLING
10 eggs
3 1/4 cups sugar
1 1/2 tablespoons grated lemon rind
2 cups fresh lemon juice (about 12 lemons)
8 tablespoons unbleached flour
2 1/2 tablespoons baking powder

1. Preheat oven to 350°F.

2. To make the crust, slice the cold butter into small pieces. In a large bowl combine the flour and confectioners' sugar.

3. Cut in the butter pieces with two knives or a pastry blender until the mixture resembles coarse oatmeal.

4. Press this mixture evenly into the bottom of an ungreased 11 x 17 x 1-inch pan.

5. Bake for about 18 to 20 minutes or until golden around the edges. The center will be only partially baked.

6. While the crust is baking, mix the filling.

7. In a large bowl whisk together the eggs and sugar. Add the grated lemon rind and juice and beat for about 5 minutes. The batter should be smooth, light and golden yellow.

8. Combine the flour and baking powder and whisk this mixture into the beaten egg mixture.

9. To avoid spilling, it's easier to pour the filling into the crust when it's still in the oven. Use a ladle or large measuring cup and pour the batter onto the crust. Fill right to the top.

10. Bake for about 25 minutes. Cool before cutting into squares. Store in the refrigerator. Just before serving, dust with confectioners' sugar.

MAKES AT LEAST 24

◆ Strawberry Rhubarb Pie ◆

◆ ◆ ◆ ◆ ◆

From spring through summer, you'll find racks of strawberry rhubarb pies coming out of the oven at **The Black Dog Bakery**. Not overly sweet, the combination of ripe strawberries and tart rhubarb stalks makes it an ideal summer dessert ~ especially served with rich vanilla ice cream.

PASTRY

2 cups all-purpose flour
1 teaspoon salt
3/4 cup vegetable shortening
4 to 5 tablespoons ice water

Before placing finished pie in oven:
1/2 cup heavy cream
2 tablespoons coarse sugar,
    also known as sanding sugar

1. Combine flour and salt in a medium bowl.

2. Use a pastry blender or two table knives to cut the shortening into the flour until the shortening/flour mixture looks like large rice grains. Sprinkle on the cold water, blending with a fork, until the dough is just moist enough to hold together.

3. Shape into a smooth ball, protect with plastic wrap, and refrigerate until ready to use.

4. If you'd like to use a food processor, pulse together the flour and the salt, then drop the shortening into the flour in small pieces. Pulse 3 or 4 times to achieve a grainy mixture. Add the ice water and pulse 3 or 4 times until a dough ball forms. Chill and reserve as above.

PIE FILLING

3/4 pound rhubarb
3 cups strawberries
3/4 cup water
1 cup granulated sugar

1/4 teaspoon nutmeg
1/2 teaspoon grated lemon rind
1/4 cup cornstarch

1. Prepare your pastry and refrigerate it. Preheat the oven to 425°F.

2. Wash all the fruit. Chop the rhubarb into 1-inch pieces and hull and slice the strawberries into halves or quarters, depending on their size. Put the prepared fruit into two separate bowls.

3. In a saucepan or kettle, combine the rhubarb, 1/2 cup water, sugar, nutmeg and lemon rind. Bring to a boil and simmer for 2 minutes.

4. In a small bowl or jar, mix together the cornstarch and ¼ cup water until thoroughly combined.

5. Stir the cornstarch mixture into the simmering rhubarb and cook until you have a thick, clear sauce. This only takes a minute or two; the rhubarb should be only partially cooked. Remove from heat and fold in the strawberries until they are completely covered. Cool completely.

6. Once your filling is made, cut the pastry ball into two sections. On a lightly floured surface, roll one out into a large circle about ⅛-inch thick and 12 inches in diameter.

7. Carefully place the dough circle into an 8-inch pie pan. Don't stretch the dough. Lift it and let it ease into the pan. Trim the excess around the edge, leaving about a ½-inch strip.

8. Fill with cooled strawberry-rhubarb mixture. Roll out the remaining dough into the same size circle as before and cut into ½-inch strips. Interweave strips to create lattice crust. Trim to match lower crust, folding and pressing firmly around the edges to seal.

9. Brush the strips and pie edge with heavy cream and sprinkle with 2 tablespoons of coarse sanding sugar.

10. Place pie on a lined baking sheet in oven. Bake for 10 minutes at 425°F and then reduce the heat to 375°F and continue baking for about 50 minutes or until crust is golden brown.

11. Cool on rack. Serve slices with a scoop of rich vanilla ice cream.

SERVES 6

◆ Blueberry Bread Pudding ◆
WITH LEMON SAUCE

◆ ◆ ◆ ◆ ◆

Blueberries are one of the great treats of summer whether eaten out of hand, sprinkled on cereal, or baked in pies. Now we discover that eating blueberries leaves us with more than a purple tongue. Science has found that these little berries offer antioxidants to protect us from stress and even help our memories and fight the aging process. Here's an easy bread pudding featuring these delicious and beneficial treats.

PUDDING

3 cups milk
1 cup light cream
¾ cup white sugar
¼ cup brown sugar
¼ teaspoon salt
4 cups day-old white bread cut into approximately ½-inch cubes

3 whole eggs
2 egg yolks
1 tablespoon cinnamon
1 cup fresh or frozen blueberries
1 Granny Smith apple, peeled, cored and sliced
1 tablespoon vanilla extract

1. Preheat oven to 350°F and butter the sides and bottom of a 9 x 13-inch baking pan.

2. Combine milk and light cream in saucepan; bring just to a boil. Remove from heat.

3. Combine sugars, salt and cinnamon in a large bowl. Toss in bread pieces to coat.

4. Lightly beat together the eggs and extra yolks and add to the large bowl. Add blueberries, apple, the hot creamy milk mixture and vanilla. Stir to combine.

5. Allow mixture to sit for about five minutes. Pour into the prepared pan.

6. Choose a shallow pan large enough to hold the baking pan (a small roasting pan is a good choice), and place your filled bread pudding pan into it. Pour boiling water into the larger pan so that it comes about halfway up the side of the other. Place in oven and bake the bread pudding in this water bath for about an hour, adding water if necessary. This procedure keeps the custard-like texture of the pudding from becoming tough. Remove from water bath and let bread pudding sit for approximately one-half hour before serving.

7. Serve warm with lemon sauce on the side.

SERVES 8 TO 10

LEMON SAUCE

$1/3$ cup sugar
1 tablespoon cornstarch
1 cup water
$2 1/2$ tablespoons soft butter
$1/2$ teaspoon grated lemon rind
$1 1/2$ tablespoons fresh lemon juice
$1/8$ to $1/4$ teaspoon salt

1. Combine sugar, cornstarch and water in a double boiler over boiling water until thickened.

2. Remove from heat and add remaining ingredients one at a time. Stir and adjust seasoning.

3. Serve warm with bread pudding.

YIELDS: $1 1/2$ CUPS

◆ Apple Crisp ◆

◆ ◆ ◆ ◆ ◆

If you're looking for fresh produce on the Vineyard, one great destination is Morning Glory Farm in Edgartown, operated by Jim and Debbie Athearn, whose family has lived on the Island for many generations. Known Island-wide for their commitment to farming and raising quality produce, they supply The Black Dog with everything from corn and strawberries to fresh herbs and cabbage. On cool summer mornings (or in early fall), you'll catch the scent of warm cider as you approach their red barn. It's a great place to get apples and make this pure comfort food ~ apple crisp. Whether you serve it warm with a generous scoop of rich vanilla ice cream or chilled with a mound of whipped cream ~ it's the best, a perennial favorite for over twenty years at The Black Dog. Why not get your apple-a-day the apple crisp way, at least once in a while.

10 Granny Smith or other tart cooking apples
1 tablespoon fresh lemon juice
1 tablespoon ground cinnamon
1/2 teaspoon ground nutmeg
1 teaspoon kirsch (optional)
3 1/2 cups sugar

3 cups all-purpose flour
1 1/2 teaspoons baking powder
a pinch of salt
3 eggs
1/2 cup unsalted butter, melted

1. Preheat the oven to 350°F. Peel, core and slice the apples in thick slices. Place these slices in a large bowl and toss with the lemon juice.

2. In a small bowl, mix together the cinnamon, nutmeg, kirsch and 1/2 cup of the sugar. Add the sugar mixture to the apples and toss to coat thoroughly. Set the apples aside while preparing the crumb topping. The apples will release some juice while waiting.

3. In another bowl, combine the remaining sugar with the flour, baking powder and salt. Make a well in the center and crack the eggs into this space. Mix the dry mixture with the eggs. Use your hands to complete the mixing, and you will achieve a better crumb-like consistency.

4. Pack a 9 x 13-inch pan with the apple mixture. Be sure to spread the mixture evenly, especially into the corners. Sprinkle the topping mixture over the pan, totally covering the apples. Then pour the melted butter evenly over the top.

5. Bake until the topping is golden, about 35 to 40 minutes.

6. Serve warm with ice cream or cool with whipped cream (see page 199).

SERVES 8 TO 10

◆

Index